the
CAMPING
book

the CAMPING book

Ed and Kate Douglas

recipes from Sue Hughes

London, New York, Melbourne,
Munich, and Delhi

Editor Claire Tennant-Scull
Designer William Hicks
Managing Editor Dawn Henderson
Managing Art Editor Christine Keilty
Senior Production Editor Jen Woodcock
Senior Production Controller Mandy Inness
Creative Technical Support Sonia Charbonnier
Photography Graham Ray, Gary Ombler,
and Kate Whitaker

First published in Great Britain in 2009
by Dorling Kindersley Limited
80 Strand, London WC2R 0RL

A CIP catalogue record for this book is
available from the British Library.

ISBN: 978 1 4053 4120 2

Colour reproduction: Colourscan, Singapore
Printed and bound: Hung Hing Printing Group Ltd., China

Discover more at
www.dk.com

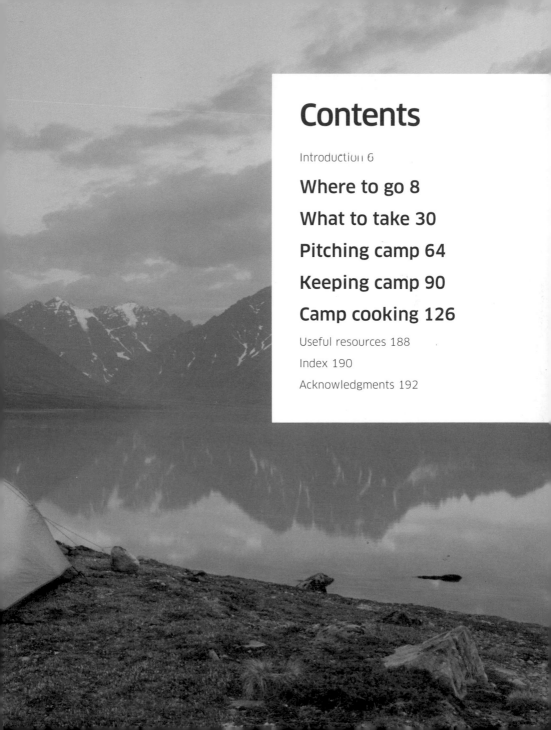

Contents

Introduction

Once upon a time we all went camping. Or rather, that's just how everyone lived. Sleeping under the stars or in rudimentary shelters, foraging for food and drinking water straight out of rivers, these are things we humans did to survive for almost all our history.

These days, being outside and living alongside nature is a trick too many of us have forgotten. But when we gather round a fire at night in the great outdoors, we're doing something our forebears did for thousands of generations.

We're not suggesting you might like to try living like one of our hunter-gatherer forebears. But there's no doubt about it. Going camping and all that entails can be deeply satisfying. In our family, we've discovered that it's the best way to spend time with those closest to us. And luckily for us, it's no longer a matter of just surviving. With all the technology and know-how at our disposable, camping can be as luxurious or simple as anyone chooses to make it.

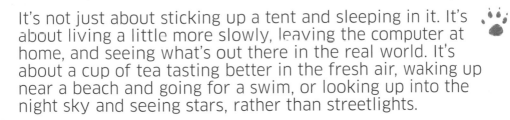

It's not just about sticking up a tent and sleeping in it. It's about living a little more slowly, leaving the computer at home, and seeing what's out there in the real world. It's about a cup of tea tasting better in the fresh air, waking up near a beach and going for a swim, or looking up into the night sky and seeing stars, rather than streetlights.

Since we started camping as children, a lot has changed. Tents are easier to put up, sleeping mats are much more comfortable, and there's a whole range of stuff out there to make camping less of a chore. But perhaps the biggest recent change is that we're all now so much more mobile.

This gives camping a marvellous spontaneity, and the fact that it's also cheap means you can take advantage of a good weather forecast and escape the speed and stress of modern living at the drop of a hat. Even if the weather's bad, it doesn't really matter. You can snuggle down in a sleeping bag, and just listen to the rain on the tent.

Ed Douglas.

Where to go

There's no one "right" way to go camping. What kind of tent you buy and where you take it it depends on who you are, and what you want to do when you get there. You may want a fully appointed campsite, a luxurious yurt, or an empty beach. Here are some of the options.

What type of camping?

Why do you want to go camping? Are you looking for a cheap family holiday? Or do you want to get far away from it all, camping wild in the hills? Once you've decided what you want from your camping experience, then you can start to think about where to go and what you'll need. Make a list of all the different factors that have to be considered before you spend money on tents and other equipment. Here are some things to think about:

Ask yourself:

🏕 **Do you want to get away from it all?** If you're looking to commune with nature, think about going wild.

🏕 **What kind of campsite would you prefer?** Some campsites will have all sorts of facilities such as showers, shops, play areas for children, and even swimming pools. But they will probably be busy. Some are highly organised, with shower blocks and numbered pitches for your tent. Others are little more than fields where you can pitch your tent wherever the fancy takes you.

🏕 **What time of year will you be camping?** Just summer? Or spring and autumn too? This will affect the quality of tent you buy, and the thickness of your sleeping bag.

🏕 **How many people will you be sharing a tent with?** Will they be adults or older children and will they need their own separate compartments? Or will you be taking young children and want to stay together in one large space?

How can you travel light? If you plan on doing without a car, and moving from campsite to campsite, then you'll need the lightest, smallest, and least gear you can get away with. There are tents designed for one person that weigh less than 1½ kilograms (4lbs). You'll need this kind of equipment that allows you to go backpacking, carrying all you need in one rucksack.

Will you fit everything in the car? If you plan on camping out of a car, then you're going to need enough space to carry all your stuff plus your regular number of passengers. Having a small vehicle won't stop you, but it's something to bear in mind when choosing a tent.

How are you going to eat? Do you want to cook over the campfire? Or will you be eating out in cafés and restaurants? You could start by just using your camp as a base, then building up to a full outdoor lifestyle. Many campers find that the savings they make allow them to have more of the treats that holidays are all about. But you'll need some kind of stove, even if it's just to make tea in the morning.

How rugged are you really? If you need certain home comforts and you can carry them with you, then bring them along. Choose your campsite and equipment to suit you and your fellow campers. Don't try to turn into a survival expert overnight.

Ready for action

Going on holiday always takes a bit of planning. But when your hotel is travelling with you, it's even more important to get off to a good start.

Before you go:

🛖 **Make lists of everything that you need.** You only have to do this once, but there's a lot of stuff to take and it's easy to forget something that you'll really need.

🛖 **Try it first.** If you've never camped before, it's not a great idea to head off into the wilds for two weeks expecting things to work out. Go camping for a weekend first, or if you've got children, try the back garden.

🛖 **Think about children's safety.** Children face new risks when they're camping but you can help them to cope by showing them how. Work out a plan with your children in advance, so that they know what to do if they forget where your tent is at the campsite. Make sure they know not to eat wild foods without your supervision and to stay away from water (no matter how shallow) when they're out and about without you.

🛖 **If you go wild, know the rules.** Many national parks around the world have rules about where you can and can't camp, and sometimes limit the numbers of permits issued for camping in the wild. Some countries prohibit wild camping altogether so take care.

- **Research your campsite before you choose.** With the internet it's now possible to get a good feel for the range of facilities, and the style of different campsites.

- **Book ahead for a few days.** Reserve the first night or two, then you can reconsider your choice if necessary. Call first, and talk to the site manager.

- **If you want a campfire, make sure it's allowed.** Many of us have childhood memories of gathering around the campfire. If you're hoping to recreate that warm feeling, make sure the site you've chosen allows fires. Those that don't may allow braziers or firepits instead.

- **If you want to bring a dog, ask first.** Check the rules before you arrive. Clean up after your dog and keep it on a leash if you're asked to. Make sure your dog has identification tags and is up-to-date on its shots.

- **Make sure you have a good map.** You'll need to know the area you're camping in. If you're going to go walking, you need a topographic map.

- **Follow the weather.** If severe weather is forecast, then reconsider your plans. And if you can avoid it, don't arrive at a new campsite after dark. Arrive early enough to put your tent up in daylight.

Car camping

For most of us, most of the time, the convenience of just loading all our gear into a car and taking off is impossible to resist. You can even take the kitchen sink, if you want, or at least a washing-up bowl.

• People who go camping are often also concerned about the environment. If you can't avoid taking your car, you can make sure it's properly maintained and that your tyre pressures are correct. At least then you'll be saving petrol.

• Take a look at your car's size. Do this before you buy your tent. Some family-sized tents take up a lot of room. You're also going to need bedding, cooking gear, and a lot of other stuff. If you don't want to buy a new car, consider using a rack, or else purchase camping gear that fits in the car you've got.

• Find out if the campsite you're heading for charges extra for a car. More informal campsites may just be a field. You don't need an off-road vehicle to reach a pitch at this kind of site, but you should be confident about driving off-road.

• Before you start loading the car, gather everything together in one place and check it off against a list.

• Try to put the things you'll need first, like the tent, in last, on top of your luggage.

Make sure that everything will fit in your car, as well as the passengers.

Going light

Not everyone wants to be tied to a vehicle, or to a crowded campsite. Hiking from campsite to campsite carrying your gear – backpacking – is a rewarding way to see the countryside, and environmentally satisfying. Putting up a tent in a wild location, assuming it is legal and you follow a code of conduct to leave no trace, is a beautiful experience that everyone should try at least once.

• If you're carrying all your equipment around, you'll want it to be as light as possible. There is a wide range of specialist lightweight gear available.

• You'll need to be fit if you're going to carry your tent and sleeping bag. Get used to carrying a heavier pack before you embark on a long trip.

• If you're walking between campsites then map-reading skills are paramount. You really do need to know where you are.

• Check whether it's legal for you to go wild camping in the area you want to visit.

• Be aware that wild camping on your own, particularly for a woman, can be hazardous.

Sheltered by trees, this tent is situated at a safe distance from the water beyond

Glamping

The camping world can seem just a little too nylon at times. There are gizmos and widgets for every eventuality, but not, it sometimes seems, much style. If you're one of those people who like their environment to have a touch of glamour, then don't let camping get in your way. Combine the two and indulge in a little "glamping".

• Find a site with unusual tents, like tipis or Mongolian yurts, they may even have wood-burning stoves inside them. Often made of canvas, these structures are a luxurious option.

• Bring lots of cosy luxuries, like pillows and cushions, or even a sheepskin rug.

• A few candles (properly shielded of course) can add lots of romance to the outdoor life.

• Decorate your tent. Tents can feature tinsel, flags, and even fairy lights. It's a great way to make your temporary abode easily recognisable in a big campsite. With a little fishing twine, some sticks and a few objets trouvés you can make mobiles too.

• Bringing a few luxuries, like a favourite coffee pot, or a few (expendable) china cups or wine glasses is a great way to reward yourself for living outside.

Beautiful and practical. Yurts can be surprisingly luxurious inside.

Full facilities

Right at the other end of the scale from wild camping, the most sophisticated sites are essentially holiday complexes, where people sleep in tents rather than rooms. Pitches will be manicured and numbered, there may be a café, there will certainly be a shop, and you'll most likely be sharing the site with caravans or RVs – recreational vehicles. If all that sounds more built-up than the natural experience you were looking for, then perhaps it's best you go elsewhere. But for kids, this kind of camping experience can be a huge success.

• More sophisticated sites are often more expensive, but they come with a wide range of facilities, like swimming pools and tennis courts, particularly in continental Europe.

• If you don't think cooking outside is much of a holiday, then having catering on site is convenient.

• Some people are concerned about security while camping, not only for their property, but themselves too. Sites with more facilities have more staff, more rules, and will also monitor and control access to the site more carefully.

A home from home may be what you're looking for in a holiday campsite.

Functional sites

These are more natural than full-facility sites, and are often little more than a field or open space with a toilet and shower block. Some may have numbered pitches, but mostly you'll be able to camp where you want, giving you more choice and freedom. There will be fewer rules and fewer people, although when this kind of site does get crowded, it can take patient negotiation between neighbours if one group wants to sleep and another wants to stay up late.

• Functional sites often allow you more space, because you're not restricted to a defined pitch.

• With fewer people and less landscaping, functional sites are much better places to see wildlife.

• You are more likely to be allowed a fire or a firepit at a functional site, but always check first.

• They may be basic, but it's easy to tell which functional sites are well managed, and which are not. Toilet blocks are welcome, especially if you have children, but only if they're cleaned regularly, so inspect them before you decide to stay.

Harmonious relations with your camp neighbours are essential on a site like this.

Festival camping

Once upon a time, young people started camping with the scouts or girl guides. These days it's more likely their first experience of life under canvas will be at a music festival. Sleeping outside is all part of the appeal of a great weekend, but the rules for camping are a little different.

• Think carefully before taking an expensive mountain tent to a festival. Discount camping stores have very cheap alternatives. It doesn't matter what happens to a cheap tent, and unless you go to festivals every weekend, it will suffice.

• Take a duffle bag on wheels, or something similar, to get your camping gear to the venue, since you won't be able to park there.

• Get a firm fix on the location of the toilet block. Don't camp too far away, but make sure you're both upwind and uphill of it.

• Security at festivals can be unreliable. Don't leave valuables in your tent, and don't bring expensive stoves or sleeping bags.

• Finding your tent in the dark when you've been partying can be confusing and infuriating. Paint, decorate, or name your shelter to find it quickly.

Earplugs may be essential if you are to get any sleep in such cosy conditions.

On the beach

Just about the most romantic thing you can do in your entire life is to spend a night sleeping on a remote beach in mid summer with a significant other. Dozing off to the sounds of waves breaking with the embers of a driftwood fire glowing nearby is something everyone should do at least once. Clearly, the onus is on you to keep the beach clean, but there are other tips to follow:

• Sleeping on a beach really only works on soft sand.

• Check the weather forecast.

• Make sure you know exactly where the high-tide mark is, unless you want to get wet.

• Beach fires are magical, but keep things discreet and go easy on the amount of wood used.

• Bedding will get damp on the outside when dew falls. Don't worry about it, because you'll be warm inside your sleeping bag or under a duvet. It's part of the fun.

• Dog mess is bad enough on a beach. Yours is a whole lot worse. If you camp wild, leave no trace.

When you leave, make sure the beach is the same paradise that you found.

Busking it

Just because you're going camping doesn't mean you have to sleep in a tent. Sometimes the most unlikely locations can turn out to be the best. From slumbering under an upturned boat in the south of France, to borrowing an old goatherd's shack high in Morocco's Atlas mountains, the unexpected can often create the most magic. Make sure, though, that you respect the local laws on trespassing, especially if the locals are armed.

• If the weather's good, and you're somewhere remote, you don't need anything, just a sleeping mat and a sleeping bag.

• Many mountain ranges have simple structures built for hikers, or disused farm buildings in wild locations, like bothies in Scotland or the more remote mountain huts in the Alps.

• In countries like New Zealand and the United States, there's a well-developed system of huts on long-distance trails.

• With a tarpaulin, you can use a wall or even a tree to provide shelter. With two strong trees, you can sleep in a hammock.

• Humans have been sleeping in caves forever. Why not try it yourself?

It's surprising how little humans really need, for a night or two, at least.

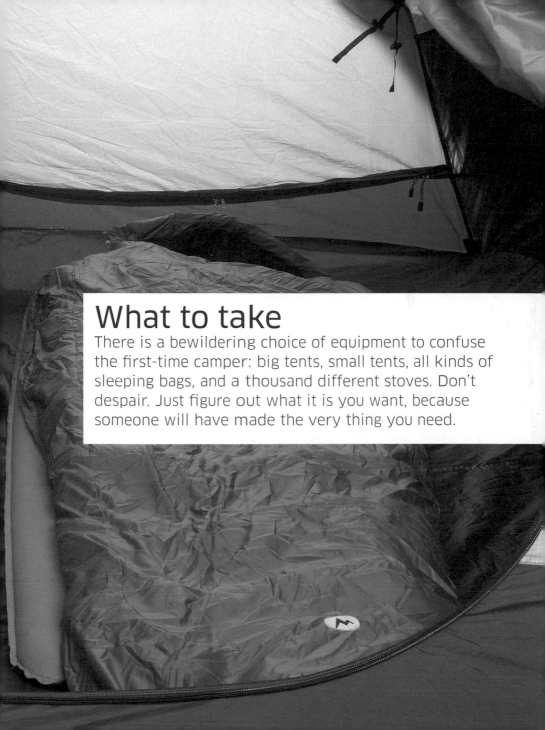

What to take

There is a bewildering choice of equipment to confuse the first-time camper: big tents, small tents, all kinds of sleeping bags, and a thousand different stoves. Don't despair. Just figure out what it is you want, because someone will have made the very thing you need.

Buying a tent: first steps

It's not quite as bad as buying a house, but figuring out what kind of tent you need can seem confusing. Don't look at a tent until you've considered some key questions:

Before you buy, ask yourself:

⟍ **How many people will use it?** One? Two? Three? A family?

⟍ **Will you be sharing with kids?** Do you want a family tent with separate sleeping quarters? Or will the children have their own tent? Do you need to be able to stand up in it?

⟍ **What time of year will you be camping?** Just summer? Or will you need something cosier for the cooler months?

⟍ **Will the climate be hot or cold?** If it's a hot climate, you'll need to keep cool. If it's cold, you'll need a tent that can cope with strong winds and heavy rain.

⟍ **How will you transport it?** Will you be car camping at a site, or going light and carrying your tent on your back?

⟍ **How easy will it be to put up and pack away?** If you're backpacking you'll be putting it up and taking it down regularly and you might need to do it in bad weather.

⟍ **What level of quality do you want?** Cheaper tents won't last as long. Unless you're a very sporadic camper, invest in as much quality as you can afford.

Family tents

The modern options most appropriate for families are larger tunnel and dome tents. Frame tents are still available, but their weight, their volume when packed, and the time they take to put up undermine their appeal. Dome tents have become very popular, although some of the biggest models can be pretty complex and time-consuming in their own right. Most family tents are hybrids of dome and tunnel types.

Poles
These are among the components most likely to break or fail, particularly the elastic linking the poles together. This elastic allows you to construct the poles quickly, but it must be cherished.

Family tent

Lobby
Cooking inside is highly dangerous. If it is raining and you want to cook, either use a tarpaulin outside, or cook in the lobby, providing it's properly ventilated and large enough to accommodate the stove and the cook. A stove should never have the chance of coming into contact with tent fabric.

Colour

Darker-coloured tents block out more sunlight, so they're easier to sleep in after dawn, but they absorb more heat so they get hotter during the day. A brightly coloured tent stands out, useful for children finding you again, or for hunters spotting you from a distance.

Bedrooms

Many family tents have separate compartments. In some tents these are removable, so if you've got a young family you can remove them, and put them back when the children are older, and you all want more privacy. Check the "people rating" on these tents carefully. You'll get a more accurate figure if you can get everyone to try them out in the showroom.

Groundsheet

Most modern tents have a sewn-in groundsheet and the more expensive ones are usually better quality. Shaped like shallow baths, the groundsheets should remain waterproof even in heavy rain.

Fabric

Modern tents are made of nylon and polyester, which makes them lighter, but hotter, and prone to condensation. Unless the weather is very cold, leave a few zips undone at night to allow the air to circulate.

Mountain tents

If you camp in cold weather, or in more exposed places, then you'll need a strong tent. Ridge and geodesic tents are the best designs for this kind of situation. The geodesic's self-supporting structure means you don't have to use guy ropes in moderate weather, and their shape offers more room. If you do a lot of camping, and occasionally do so in the wild, or in bad weather, then a two or three-person geodesic tent is a very good option.

Geodesic tent

Entrance
The door is double-zipped, and can be rolled back, allowing cooking in the lobby in bad weather. There is an entrance at the other end, to stow gear. Some geodesic models also have an extended lobby for the harshest conditions.

Flysheet

The flysheet is heavier than lightweight tents, making this tent warmer, and the seams are sealed to prevent water from getting through. The better quality tents tend to have flysheets that are more durable. The guy rope attachment points have reflective strips, so you can see the guy ropes in the dark.

Poles

High-quality aluminium poles slot into brass eyelets, flexing, and combining to create a strong structure that is self-supporting, without the need to peg out guy-ropes in good weather.

Peg points

Pegs are inserted through the same nylon tape that holds the poles. The fly is then clipped to a metal or plastic loop by the pole inserts. These tapes are adjustable, so the flysheet can be tightened to make the tent warmer and more storm-proof.

Lightweight tents

If you carry your tent in a rucksack, you need it to be as light as possible. For two or three people sharing, the ideal solution is a semi-geodesic tent, (that uses three poles instead of the standard four or five) or else a tunnel tent. If you're taller, then a tunnel tent may be the better option, as they tend to be longer. Unlike a geodesic tent, they are not freestanding, and have to be pegged out securely before use, but the inner and flysheet can be erected together.

Poles
Two or three separate flexible poles form the tent's shape. Nylon tape braces inside the tent can be adjusted against the poles to give the structure strength in a cross wind.

Tunnel tent

Pegs
Tunnel tents require strong peg placements to achieve their shape. This can be a problem on very hard or stony ground.

Accommodation

The manufacturer rates this tent for three people. Although it would be a tight squeeze, that works out, for a 3kg (6lb) tent, to be just 1 kilo (2lbs) each to carry. The semi-circular shape means there is more headroom than a semi-geodesic tent.

Rear lobby

Tunnel tents are often roomier than similar sized semi-geodesic tents. The inner of this one extends right to the end.

Lobby

The entrance to this tent is surprisingly large for its light weight. It's handy if you want to store your kit inside, out of the rain. The entrance also has a rain gutter, to direct rain away from the covered area where the door is open.

Guy ropes

Because tunnel tents are vulnerable to crosswinds, make sure the guy ropes are pegged out and kept taut, especially in bad weather.

Backpacking tents

If you want complete freedom to carry your tent where you want, by yourself, then a traverse hoop design is an excellent option. This tent weighs 1.8kg (just under 4lbs), a manageable weight for a solo hiker or cyclist, and can fit two people in reasonable comfort. These tents can feel exposed in bad weather, however, and have to be pegged well in a cross wind.

Guy points
Because of the single-pole design, the flysheet has to be guyed out for the tent to be stable.

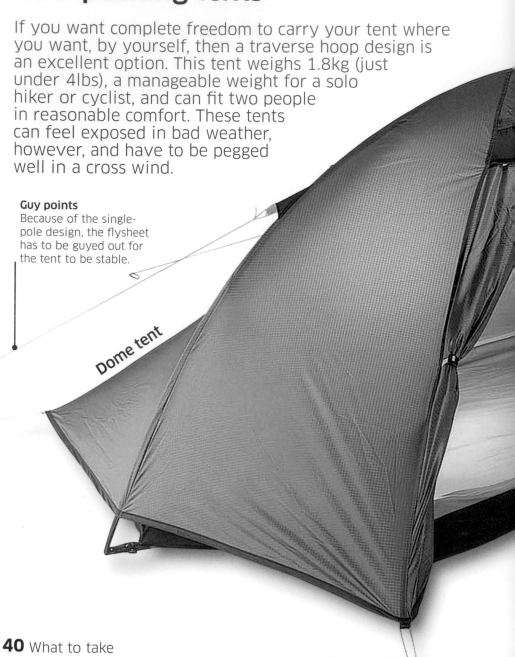

Dome tent

Vents
Condensation in a small tent can be a problem, as it's far more likely you'll brush against the walls where it collects. Vents in this tent aim to reduce the problem.

Pitching options
Clever design means you can remove the inner altogether for camping in fine weather, to cut down weight further.

Pole
A traverse hoop tent is like a tarp, but with the hoop providing tension along a diagonal with the other corners pegged out.

Inner
The inner tent is put up together with the flysheet, making this tent very fast to erect. Nylon tapes attached to the other corners provide tension to form its rectangular shape.

Something to sleep on

Although sewn-in tent groundsheets are waterproof these days, they don't offer much insulation or comfort. Lie down on one in a sleeping bag, and unless you're used to sleeping on a hard floor, you'll soon feel uncomfortable. More importantly, you will also lose a great deal of your body heat during the night through conduction. What you sleep on will definitely solve the insulation problem. What it may not do is make you comfortable. It's more than possible to get a great night's sleep in a tent, but how lightweight an option you can tolerate depends on how you feel about hard surfaces. There are four main options:

Closed-cell foam mat

These require no effort to use. Simply lay them on the floor and lie down. They offer excellent insulation. This model is good for three seasons, but you would require something slightly thicker in winter. The ridged pattern on its surface is surprisingly comfortable for a mat which is just 2cm (¾in) thick.

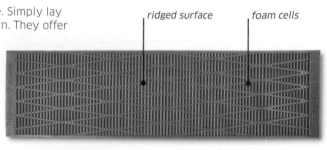

ridged surface   *foam cells*

Open-cell foam mat

These incorporate a foam mat enclosed in a nylon sheath and sealed with a valve. You open the valve and blow air into the mat until it is inflated and then close the valve. This offers a great deal of comfort for little weight. The valves are prone to failure, but some brands offer lifetime warranties. Narrower and shorter versions are available for lightweight camping.

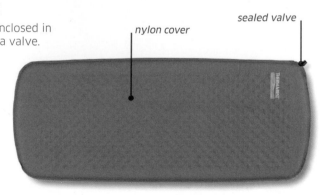

nylon cover   *sealed valve*

Airbed

These offer excellent insulation and comfort, and are often cheaper than open-cell foam mats. But they are heavy and require pumping up. If you take this option, then don't forget to bring a pump. Electric models are available if you don't want to bother with a foot-pump. This model has an integrated pump.

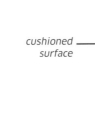

cushioned surface

inflation valve

Camp bed

These are much less popular for camping than they once were, but a camp bed does have distinct advantages. First, they don't puncture, and if you get one that's sturdy and durable that you feel comfortable using, then you are guaranteed a good night. They can also be used as daybeds, for dozing in the sunshine outside.

flexible fabric

folding legs

Something to sleep in

If you feel constricted in a sleeping bag, it's fine to go camping with your duvet or blankets, and a sheet. Some manufacturers now make duvet-style sleeping bags so you can have all the comfort of home in your tent. You may find, however, that your duvet takes up a lot of room in the car, and carrying them for any distance is impractical.

Natural or synthetic?

There are many factors to consider when choosing the right bag for you. Whether you're off for a mountain adventure or beach-side break, think before you buy.

Down sleeping bags	Synthetic sleeping bags
Either natural goose or duck feathers are used to line down sleeping bags. The quality of down sleeping bags is measured on a temperature, or "fill rating" system, which peaks at "800 Fill Down" – the warmest.	*Materials such as PrimaLoft or Spirafil, and which are used to stuff household duvets, are also used in synthetic sleeping bags. Their properties are different to natural down bags as shown below here.*
Warmer per gram of filling.	Needs more weight of filling for a similar level of warmth.
Loses its shape when wet. Loses insulating properties when wet. Takes a long time to dry.	Maintains its shape when wet. Maintains most of its insulating properties when wet. Dries relatively quickly.
Lightweight. Will pack smaller for backpacking.	Heavy. Cannot be compressed as much as a down sleeping bag.
When not in use, is best stored in a large mesh bag, to allow air to circulate, so can take up more space.	Takes up less space when stored. Not affected by storage.
Expensive.	Inexpensive.

Summer camp

Summer camping sleeping bags are very cheap, and are made in roomy, box shapes for comfort, making them the ideal choice for car camping, festivals, or the beach.

HOOD
This has a drawstring, allowing you to cinch the top of the bag around your head on cold nights, trapping the warm air.

LINER
Nylon fabric inside your sleeping bag can be sticky and uncomfortable, especially in summer. This bag has a removable polyester and cotton inner.

WEIGHT
This sleeping bag weighs almost 2kg, (4lb 8oz) too heavy and bulky to be much use in backpacking. A down-filled sleeping bag offering the same insulation would weigh less than half this amount.

FILLING
Cheaper sleeping bags use artificial fibres as their filling. These offer a lot of insulation but tend to be heavier. However, they are also easier to clean.

ZIP
The zip extends all the way round the bag, allowing it to be opened completely on hot days, or combined with another to form a double. But buy one with a right zip and another with a left, if that's your plan.

SHAPE
The rectangular shape allows free movement of the legs. That means that it has colder spots, and that air can move more freely, which could be a disadvantage in lower temperatures.

3-season warmth

If you're doing anything more than summer car camping, such as backpacking or sleeping in colder weather, then a good sleeping bag is essential. Choose here between synthetic and natural insulation.

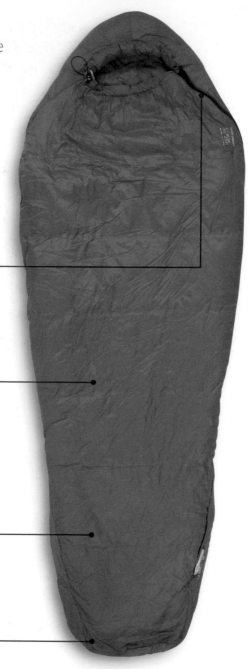

ZIP
This bag has a two-way zip. In summer, your feet can often be too hot while your torso needs insulating. A two-way zip allows you to ventilate the bottom of the bag.

FILLING
This bag has a high-quality polyester fibre filling, but weighs only 1kg (2lbs 4oz). It's a good choice for situations where a bag must be carried and might get wet, but it is still quite bulky.

TEMPERATURE RATING
Judging how warm a bag will keep you isn't precise. It depends partly on your metabolism. Bag manufacturers use a range of scales, comparing seasons or temperatures. This bag has been rated to 0°C, making it appropriate for spring, summer, and autumn at low altitudes.

SHAPE
Unlike a rectangular design, this bag has been tapered to fit snugly around the legs. You lose some comfort but the bag is considerably warmer.

HOOD

The top of the bag can be closed around the head, sealing warm air inside. And because the bag is over 2m (6ft 6in) in length, even tall people will feel comfortable.

ZIP

The two-way zip is protected by a "baffle", a down-filled compartment that covers its whole length and prevents heat loss through this weak spot.

FILLING

This bag is filled with goose down. It offers superb insulation for its weight. Weighing only 1.1kg, it is rated down to -12°C, but packs smaller than the polyester filled bag. This makes it suitable for camping and backpacking in winter in the mountains.

BAG STRUCTURE

Because down moves around freely, it is trapped in box compartments sewn throughout the bag. This keeps the down spread evenly across your body.

Down

Natural down is a superb insulator and is lighter, longer-lasting, and more compressible than polyester fibres. But it has to be specialist-cleaned, and unlike synthetic fillings, it loses its insulating properties when wet.

Head rest

If you need extra cushioning for your head you could try a camping pillow. Most have hollow-fibre insulation and can be compressed and packed in their own stuff sack for easy storage and transportation.

Something to sleep in **47**

What to cook on

Camping stoves are more efficient and convenient than cooking on an open fire. There are two kinds of burner, pressurised and unpressurised, and several kinds of fuel: gas, most commonly a propane and butane mix, or either one on its own; liquid fuels, like kerosene also known as paraffin, gasoline, or petrol, white gas, or methylated spirits; and solid fuels (which are cheap, but slow). You won't be able to fly with stove fuel, so check that your destination country can supply the fuel you need.

Gas twin burner with grill

• This kind of stove is most appropriate for car camping, and recreates the easy convenience of cooking at home.

• There are two burners, meaning you can cook more complex meals, and a grill for toast or bacon.

• Big gas stoves tend to have big cylinders, which will last for a week or so of camping, but they must be refilled at a camping outfitter's. Make sure you know where you can refill your canister. Bigger campsites will often stock it.

Connecting valve

Metal canister

Flame controls

Backpacking gas stove

• Gas is also a good fuel to carry in a rucksack. This stove only weighs 150g (5½ oz) and will boil a litre (1¾pts) of water in under 4 minutes.

• It also has a self-ignition system, so you don't need matches or a lighter.

• While small stoves are very light and convenient, they are also rather unstable, particularly with a full saucepan on top. You must make sure that the stove is properly positioned on the ground before lighting it.

• Some backpacking gas stoves now come with a heat exchanger system which doubles their efficiency and decreases the time it takes to boil a litre of water to around a minute. These stoves are also twice the price.

Pan stand

Small burner

Self ignition

Gas canister

Small car-camping gas stove

• This cooker is a cost-effective compromise between a backpacking stove and a large car-camping stove. Its square shape makes it very stable.

• The stove has an integral butane cylinder, which means there are no connecting hoses, but the canister will need changing more often than a larger bottle. It also has a self-ignition system. Be aware that these can wear out.

Wind shield

Grill underneath

Stoves and barbecues

Parents constantly remind their children about the dangers of a kitchen stove. In camping, you take your stove with you, and it is, if anything, even more dangerous. A lot of outdoor gear is flammable, especially tents, so never cook inside one, and only cook inside the lobby of a tent if it's well ventilated. Igniting a stove can produce tall flames unexpectedly, so never light one underneath anything. Always test a new stove at home, outside, before taking it camping so you can resolve any problems then.

Methylated spirit stove

• This stove is unpressurised and burns methylated spirits. This makes it convenient and safer, but the heat output is lower than other stoves.

• It comes with an integral windshield to protect the flame if it's breezy. Other stoves lack this, although windshields are easily improvised, or can be bought.

• The stove comes with two pans that integrate into the stove for convenience, and provide a case for the stove when it's packed into a rucksack. The whole system weighs just 860g (less than 2lbs).

• Unpressurised stoves are not recommended for use at higher altitudes..

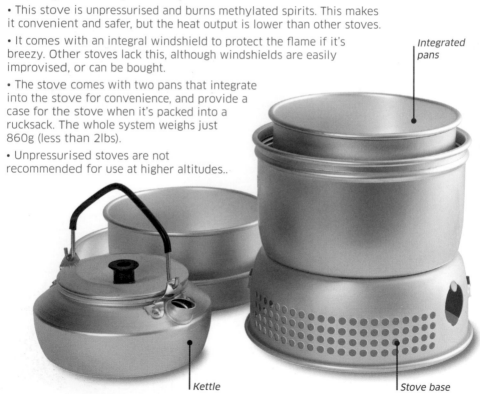

Integrated pans

Kettle

Stove base

Multi-fuel stove

• For many backpackers, this kind of stove is very popular. The burner itself weighs just 85g, (3oz) and can use a range of fuels such as white gas, unleaded gasoline, and kerosene, but not alcohol.

• The fuel is stored in a bottle, which you pressurise before the stove is lit. As the fuel is released into the atmosphere, it vapourises and then burns.

• Pressurised liquid fuel stoves are highly efficient, boil water quickly, and work well at altitude.

• Burning liquid fuel, and the additives in some fuels leaves deposits that can affect the performance of a stove. They must be cleaned and maintained regularly.

Gas burner

Pressurised gas

Heat reflector

Barbecues

• If you like barbecuing but your campsite won't allow open fires on the ground, then a portable charcoal barbecue is a good solution. More expensive gas models are also available.

• You'll need a stove, too, so make sure your vehicle is big enough to cope; barbecues can take up a lot of space.

Lighting a stove

• The smallest items are the easiest to forget. Your stove is useless without something to light it. Don't forget matches or a lighter, and preferably both.

• For backpacking, where lighting a stove is critical, you can carry storm matches which light in a strong wind and will even work after immersion in water.

Charcoal drum

Elevating legs

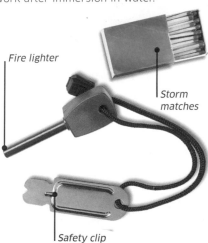

Fire lighter

Storm matches

Safety clip

Absolute essentials

As well as your basic equipment, these are the extras that you simply cannot leave home without.

A mallet will be much appreciated if you've ever tried pushing a tent peg in by hand.

Tent pegs are like small change, they just disappear, so carry some spares. Some available are made from biodegradeable plastic, so if you do lose them, they really should just disappear.

A water container saves you time, as you'll often have to camp some distance from a tap, and going back and forth to fetch water can become extremely tiresome.

Spare fuel will be needed if you're using a gas cartridge or liquid fuel that will run out after a couple of days' use, so always make sure that you have some spare.

A headtorch is very useful for freeing up both hands for tasks, and perfect for reading in bed.

A light mallet will save you hurting your hand pushing in tent pegs.

An air pump will be necessary if you're going to blow up air beds. There are foot pumps and electric versions available too.

Lanterns come in two types, electric and gas, but gas means bringing something burning into your tent. Electric LED lanterns are sufficiently bright.

A tarpaulin and poles are great if you're planning to set up a kitchen area outside your tent but don't forget to bring some spare cord to use as guy ropes.

A plastic bottle is great, so you can carry a drink during the day, and measure fluids for cooking at night.

Duct tape can repair or improve pretty much anything made for the great outdoors.

A solar panel can recharge your mobile phone or MP3 player, (if you really can't survive without them) in an eco-friendly way.

Light your way with a portable heavy-duty lantern.

Everyday essentials

Nobody wants to think too much about chores when they go on holiday, but having a list of everything you'll need to make things easier lets you get on with enjoying yourself.

A washing-up kit can be taken along without adding too much weight or bulk if you're car camping. A washing-up bowl, detergent, and gloves can make the job of cleaning dishes a lot less unpleasant.

A washing kit in a bag you can hang-up and unzip is more practical than a regular wash bag. Small bottles of soap and shampoo are great when backpacking. Hand sanitizers are particularly useful for children.

Camping towels or travel towels that dry more quickly make life so much easier.

Quick-dry camping towels get you dry in seconds, dry out in minutes, and can be rolled up into tiny bundles.

Waterproof bags should be kept handy to keep clothes dry, or store dirty clothes before washing. A dry-bag, which can be sealed, is useful for cameras or phones.

Clothes lines can be made easily enough, but outdoor stores carry handy elasticated clothes lines that work well inside tents.

A dustpan and brush will help to keep your tent tidy and sand out of your sleeping bag. Camping by a beach can result in large levels of sand getting inside your tent so keep sweeping.

A first-aid kit, well maintained and updated is essential. Check that any medicines are not out-of-date and replace as necessary (see pp108–9).

A multi-tool should be carefully stored but there are lots of small jobs where a penknife or multi-tool is useful, from cutting rope to extracting fishing hooks.

Keep a tool for every task safely stowed away in your pocket.

Optional luxuries

Popular culture says camping is for hardy types who don't mind a bit of discomfort. The best campers are those who welcome a little bit of luxury into their camping lives, and are resourceful about doing it. After all, you are on holiday.

Coffee makers For proper, fresh coffee, bring a camping cafetière or espresso maker.

Cake You can cook most things over a campfire, but cake is very hard to make successfully. Why not bring a homemade cake to share around at teatime? (See pp183-5 for inspiration.)

Wine glasses Plastic wine glasses are so much better than mugs – indulge yourself.

Rugs A tent can be transformed by a sheepskin rug.

Telescope Most of us rarely see the stars. Bring a telescope, and spend your evenings stargazing (see pp116-9).

Candles There's nothing more romantic than candlelight inside a tent. But be safe, there are special candle holders available for this very purpose. Use them.

A little luxury goes a long way when you're camping. Take a few home comforts.

Kids' camping kit

Camping is made for children. The outdoors is a classroom, playground, and home from home all rolled into one. But kids may be anxious about some aspects of what is a strange new experience, so take some time to explain some of the wild new things that might happen. Give them their very own equipment and camping goodies, along with a few well-chosen favourites from home, and you'll be halfway there. It's also worth having a dry run at a campsite a few miles away. Back gardens are fine, but the temptation of a familiar bedroom can be overwhelming at 2am.

Favourite toys, books, and games will make kids feel at home, particularly at bed time, but make sure you either watch that cuddly toy like a hawk, or keep a spare secretly stashed, in case it all goes wrong.

A torch for night time is crucial. Fresh air tends to make kids sleep deeply, but getting them to drift off is easier with the reassurance of a bedside light.

A disposable camera for making a record of early adventures is great fun, even if the pictures come out a little wonky and blurry.

Treasure boxes should be kept handy for kids to collect any amazing feathers or stones they might find, or anything else that takes their fancy.

Nature books and spotters guides for birds, insects, and flowers will give children every chance to develop their inner naturalist. Binoculars and a magnifying glass will help too.

A rucksack doesn't have to be big, or expensive, but it's very exciting for kids to have their very own bag to put their important stuff in.

Emergency rations should be kept in the rucksack in case things go awry. These will last approximately five minutes after dark, but then, that's the point.

Useful clothes

What you wear camping depends on when and where you go, and what you plan to do when you get there. That's a whole different book in itself, although keep in mind that it's often harder to dry clothes camping than it is normally. Jeans are great, but drying them is awkward. Some campsites have drying facilities, but basic sites don't. There are also a few items that people don't immediately think of that can be very useful for living in a tent.

Ponchos may not be much of a fashion statement, but they are very useful camping, especially in the middle of a summer rainstorm. They are quick to put on, and aren't constricting, which is more comfortable in warm weather. Even better, you can hold things under them, like bowls of food, a rucksack, or children.

Shawls or blankets in fine wool, or even a pashmina are perfect for cooler evenings where you don't want to struggle into a jumper or fleece. Wrap yourself up, and sit by the fire.

Wellington boots or galoshes are essential kit if you're camping in one of those parts of the world that sees regular and prolonged rain. They're great for wading through streams too.

Sandals are perfect for slipping bare feet into to cross to the toilet block. If all you've got as an alternative are trainers or walking boots, then the 2am dash becomes more of a chore. Having sandals that will handle wet conditions is even better.

Floppy hats are particularly useful for children, but everyone should have access to a hat to keep the sun off their necks and faces. Always have a light long-sleeved shirt available too.

Umbrellas, while not officially "clothes", are instant and convenient rain shelter, without having to put on a soggy raincoat. But of course you're restricted to what you can carry in one hand.

Boots and a hat will keep your feet dry and your face protected.

Packing your rucksack

With a rucksack, organisation and easy access are key. Use these essential packing tips as a guide.

Pack raingear at the top where you can get it quickly

Store essentials such as suncream, a compass, maps, and guidebooks in an outer pocket

Keep first aid items accessible

Waterproof bags should be used to store items that must stay dry, particularly spare clothing and your sleeping bag

Heaviest items should sit between your shoulder blades and as close to your back as possible

Carry your waterbottle upright where it's accessible

Store fuel bottles upright and outside the pack

Lighter items such as sleeping mats and bags should remain at the bottom of the rucksack

Put your tent in a waterproof stuff sack and strap it to the outside of your backpack

Packing your car

How you pack your car is a good personality test. The world doesn't end if you just throw everything in the back, but there are a few things you can do to make sure that things go smoothly. The most important thing is not to forget critical pieces of equipment. Tents don't work without their poles. So lay everything out near the door before loading so you can check through a list of things to take. Here are some more tips:

• Large plastic boxes are ideal for packing cooking gear and food and make loading and unloading fast.

• It doesn't really matter in what order most of your gear goes in, but do leave the tent near the very top. The first thing you'll do is put it up.

• Leave raincoats or your poncho on top of the tent, in case it's raining when your arrive.

• Make sure that your emergency roadside kit is easily accessible.

• Check visibility through the rear windscreen before you set off.

Pitching camp

With experience, choosing a campsite and setting up your tent will become second nature. But even if you are a first-time camper, there are plenty of tricks you can learn to make your camping experience more comfortable and enjoyable.

Pitching your tent: first steps

After a long drive, or a long hike, the temptation is to get the tent put up as quickly as possible. If you're only going to be staying on the site for one night, and the weather's good, it doesn't matter too much if you get it wrong. But if you're staying longer, or there's a chance of heavy rain, it's important to think clearly about where you're going to pitch your tent.

Do your research

At some functional sites, there may be restrictions about where you can camp. That's why it's worth calling ahead to find out what these are. This will mean you can get down to the business of setting yourself up as soon as you arrive at the site.

Find your pitch

If you're camping at a full-facilities site, there will be a reception area that you should report to first. You will most likely be assigned a pitch by number, in which case there are not many more decisions to make, although there should be room for negotiation if you are not happy. If you're turning up to another type of site, the choice of where exactly you'd like to pitch your tent is up to you. See opposite for key questions to ask yourself before you take the plunge, and turn to pp68–69 to see a real-life perfect pitch.

Before you pitch, ask yourself:

What are your neighbours like? If people are camping close to you, are there to party, and you are not, don't hesitate to ask for an alternative pitch.

Is there a trail or footpath nearby? Don't pitch your tent across or near a footpath or animal trail. You'll be disturbed by whoever, or whatever, uses it.

Where is your water? If you need the nearest river or stream, then camp near it, but not right by it. Standing water may attract insects, so keep more of a distance.

Is the ground flat, firm, and even? It needs to be. Don't worry too much about it being covered in grass. That grass can often conceal lumps anyway. Your mat or airbed will give you the necessary comfort.

Are there surrounding trees? They can be useful as windbreaks and for tying things to, but don't camp under hanging branches or too close to the trunk. Trees drip after a downpour and also attract lightning.

Is there a prevailing wind? Make sure you orientate your tent so that you position openings away from any strong winds. Though brisk winds will at least help to keep any insects away.

Choosing your pitch

Once you've got a rough idea of where you want to put your tent in relation to the facilities you need, other people, and possible disturbances, then it's time to take a good look at potential sites. This riverside site illustrates many of the issues that you need to consider before you even begin to take your tent out of your car or rucksack.

Ground Although there's little grass in the foreground, the earth is firm, flat, and even and also shows no evidence of becoming waterlogged. At 18 metres (60ft) from the river it should be quite safe and quiet.

Trees These are ideal as they offer some shelter from the wind, but have few overhanging branches which could break off and fall on your tent. They could also be used to tie a tarpaulin to.

Weather If there's a persistent local wind then it makes sense to put your door downwind of it, particularly if your tent is vulnerable to cross-winds.

Fireplace At the back of the pitch, nearest the river, is an established fireplace. You can see how the stones around it delineate where you can and can't burn wood. It's important to always respect these conventions.

Water The river offers a good source of running water, but check that there's no danger of flooding. It's also a risk area for children.

Fully pitched With this combination of family tent and tarpaulin, the tarp does not extend over the fireplace, which would be dangerous. Together, the tarp and tent offer a spacious amount of accommodation for a variety of activities.

Choosing your pitch **69**

Pitching your family tent

Family camping tents are larger than most, accommodating up to ten people. They should be sturdy, but will be designed for moderate rather than severe weather conditions. Although if you have young children you will probably want to be close together, look for tents that can be separated into rooms, so that some family members can have a little privacy.

1 Unpack the tent from the bag. It follows an extended dome design and is straightforward to put up, especially with two people to do it. You'll put the inner layer up first, and then add the outer one.

2 Shake out the inner approximately where you will peg out the tent. This kind of tent is self-supporting and so can be easily moved later to the best position.

Place the tent's five poles in the sleeves in the inner tent and flysheet. Put them together by matching their colour-coding to the corresponding coloured flashing on the tent sleeve.

3

4 Place the tent in your favoured location, then get inside and lie down. This will alert you to any uncomfortable lumps that might ruin your sleep. You can then peg the tent out.

5 Use a mallet for larger tents where you have to place many pegs. Or you could use stone as an alternative. Always drive the pegs in at a slight inward angle (see pp80–1).

6 Once you have put the flysheet over the tent you can decide how to organise the interior space. Here an inner wall is used to separate one end of the structure off as sleeping quarters.

7 The pitched tent. Sheltered by trees, it is pitched on level ground with plenty of ventilation and light. This will provide a comfortable base with distinct areas for sleeping and socializing.

Pitching your mountain tent

Mountain tents are a great choice for outdoor people who do a lot of car camping. Although heavier than backpacking tents, they can also be carried, and offer four-season protection so you won't have to worry about a good quality mountain tent blowing down. They aren't tall enough to stand up in, but they do have vestibules front and back for cooking and storage.

1 Take out the tent, shake out the groundsheet, and locate the poles. This geodesic tent will need to be pegged at each corner first.

2 Find the five colour coded poles in the sockets on the nylon tape at each corner, and along the side. Put the corner poles in first.

3 Find the central locking hook first. The wire gate should be closed to provide a strong fixture. When you have fixed all the locking gates, attach all the hooks to the poles.

4 Once the additional two main poles have been added, you can attach the inner, fully, and the tent's geodesic structure can clearly be seen. These crossed poles are what makes it so strong and resistant to high winds.

5 Now you can throw the fly sheet over the inner part of the tent and poles. Link the attachment points on the flysheet to the pole structure, then add the fifth pole under the flysheet to support the lobby or vestibule.

6 Attach the clips on the base of the flysheet to the rings on the tape you previously pegged out. These can then be tightened against the poles to make a really strong, wind and weather resistant structure (see pp80-1).

7 Now fully assembled. Because most mountain tents pitch the inner part first, the strength and stability of the tent comes from the crossed poles, with both the inner and outer parts of the tent working together.

Pitching your mountain tent **73**

Pitching your backpacking tent

Tents you can carry comfortably all day are by necessity going to be smaller. But this tunnel design has more than enough room for two people and their gear. One advantage is that you can put up the fly sheet and inner tent together, which is useful if it's raining. But figure out the direction of the prevailing wind as tunnels are more vulnerable to cross winds.

1 Although this tent comes in a single bag it's easy to divide its weight between two people to share the load. You will be linking the pole segments together and like most modern tent poles, they are pre-linked by elastic cord.

2 Thoroughly shake out the tent so that it achieves its full length and width. If it's windy, peg out the fly sheet at one end.

3 The pole sleeves on this tent are closed at one end, and the pole ends are asymmetric. Make sure you put the blunt, rounded end into the sleeve.

4 Put the other end into the brass hole on the nylon tapes that span the groundsheet. Then stretch the tent lengthways, peg in, and tighten the tape.

5 Fasten the inner tent to the flysheet by pushing the toggles through plastic rings. (In good weather you could remove the inner to save weight).

6 Once the pegs are in, and the tapes tightened, the guy ropes can be pegged out and tightened to give more lateral strength in a cross wind..

Pitching your lightweight tent

For those hiking long distances for days or even weeks on end, this tent is light enough to carry on your own, although it will offer enough space for two people. To save even more weight, you may wish to take only a tarpaulin and use some walking poles to support it, but this kind of tent is so light, it weighs little more than a bag of sugar, so it's worth the effort.

1 Start by removing your tent from the carry bag. The fly and inner tent of this model are erected together, a useful design feature when pitching a tent in the rain.

2 Slacken off the nylon tapes at each corner of the inner before you insert the single pole. Try to remember to do this when you take the tent down.

3 Carefully connect each segment of the pole together, taking care not to strain the elastic by letting the pole segments snap together.

4 The pole ends on this model are identical, so it doesn't matter which end you use. Gently insert it into the single pole sleeve.

5 Insert the end of the pole in the stainless steel ring in the tape. Push the pole through the sleeve, freeing bunched material as you go. Never pull the pole as it will separate the segments.

6 Now you can peg out one side of the flysheet. The pole will have to lie flat while you do this, but pulling out the opposite side of the fly sheet will work to bring the whole thing upright.

7 Once the structure is upright, stabilize the tent with the guy ropes. Use a stone to drive in the pegs if you don't want to carry a heavy mallet (see pp80-1).

Putting up a tarpaulin

In summer, when you really don't want to be inside a hot tent during the day, a tarpaulin is a useful option as a shelter. Essentially just a large square of nylon fabric, two poles at either end of a diagonal pegged out with guy ropes will give it height, and the other corners are tied off to give it width. You could do without poles and just tie it to any suitable trees, but it's much easier to put up with two people than on your own.

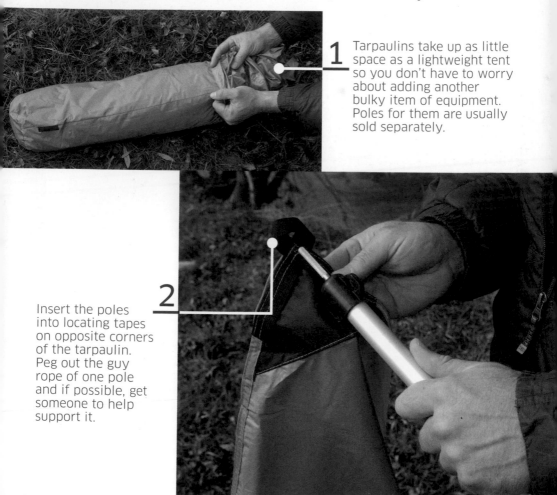

1 Tarpaulins take up as little space as a lightweight tent so you don't have to worry about adding another bulky item of equipment. Poles for them are usually sold separately.

2 Insert the poles into locating tapes on opposite corners of the tarpaulin. Peg out the guy rope of one pole and if possible, get someone to help support it.

3 Now insert the other pole and stretch the fabric out. The poles should sit leaning slightly out for stability. Once these are secure, peg out the second guy rope.

4 Using nylon cord and some useful knots (see pp82–3), tie off the guy rope to a nearby tree. You can also use a peg in the ground and a guy rope to stretch them out.

5 The final structure should look something like this. A tarpaulin will offer good protection from the sun, and any rain will run off at the corners. You can use it to cook under with a camp stove (as long as you ensure that the flame is nowhere near the fabric), but never light an open fire beneath it.

Troubleshooting

Although putting up tents isn't complex, you'll rarely do it perfectly. This doesn't matter most of the time, and a wonky groundsheet isn't the end of the world. But if rain is forecast, or strong winds, then a properly erected tent becomes more critical. If the flysheet and inner aren't properly aligned, then they can come into contact and water can penetrate the inner. Loose guy ropes or slack corners will rattle in a high wind, and may even fail in severe weather. Here are a few solutions:

Creased flysheet

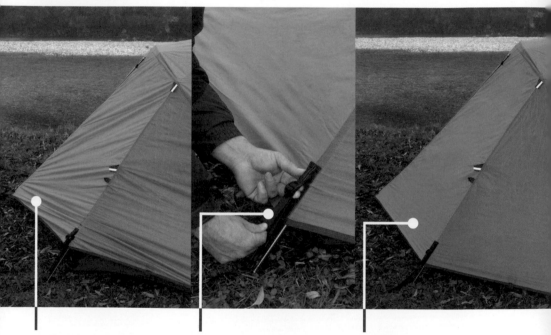

Problem The creased flysheet of this mountain tent has left a gap between the bottom of the flysheet and the ground. In driving rain or strong winds, this could be a weakness.

Adjustment Pull the tape taut through this buckle in order to adjust the flysheet. This will straighten out the creases and bring the flysheet down further over the inner.

Result The flysheet now looks smooth and even around the back of the tent. If a tent looks perfect, then you know that all the design features that make it strong are working.

Wrinkled groundsheet

Problem The wrinkled groundsheet in this lightweight tent means that the sleeping area is reduced. It also indicates that the tent is not properly pitched.

Adjustment You need to adjust the tape attachments at either corner of the groundsheet to smooth it out, and to tighten the tension on the single hoop.

Result Now the groundsheet has achieved its full size. In a small tent, this can make the difference between a good night's sleep and a bad one.

Unaligned poles

Problem This tunnel tent is uneven, because the poles aren't on the ground in a straight line. The flysheet is creased and the tent won't spread to its full width inside, limiting space.

Adjustment Adjust the tape attached to the pole sleeve, so that the centre pole can be brought back in line. These tapes run the width of the tent. Keep them taut for best results.

Result The diagonal creases have gone and the middle pole is properly aligned with the other two. Inside, the groundsheet is flat and the inner is as wide as it can be.

Some useful knots

You don't have to be a nautical whiz to go camping, but there are a few knots that are very useful for everyday tasks around the campsite, like tying up tarpaulins, attaching guy ropes to flysheets, or fixing a swing. Here are four knots it's worth practising on a rainy afternoon. If you can, use rope rather than string to learn a knot. String is too fiddly and you won't be able to see what you've created.

Fisherman's knot

Especially useful for repairing snapped guy ropes, this can be used to tie together two lengths of rope, even if they are of different thicknesses. A reef knot can also be used, but has to be kept under tension.

Taut-line or Tent hitch

Useful for attaching guy ropes, this is an adjustable loop knot that can be slackened off and shortened easily to maintain the correct tension.

Start with the working end of the rope. Take it around a large loop and then pass the working end through.

Take the working end over the standing piece and through the loop. Then over, and through the loop again.

Pass the working end around the standing part and push it through the loop. Pull the standing end to tension the knot.

Bowline

The usefulness of the bowline lies in being able to pass a rope around a tree or through a metal ring and tie it off securely and simply, so it's great for tying tarpaulins.

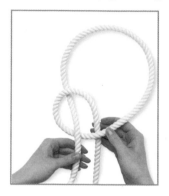  

Take the long working end of the rope in your left hand and pass it through a large loop.

Now pull the working end through the loop and pass it behind the large loop.

Pass the working part up through the smaller loop then pull on both ends to tighten and secure.

Clove hitch

Another commonly used knot, this one is really useful for fixing a tarpaulin line around a stake or branch.

Make two large loops and hold them side by side. The piece on top of each crossing should be the right strand of rope.

Holding the loops in each hand, bring the right loop over so that it is positioned on top of the left loop.

Pass the crossing turns over the end of a pole. Pull on both ends of the rope to tighten the knot around the pole.

Kitchen knowhow

One of the great pleasures of camping is good food made and consumed outdoors. There's something about eating in the open air that puts your taste buds on top form. The "kitchen" quickly becomes the focus for camp living. So where should you put it? If the weather's fine, it's easy, you can cook outside. But if it's raining then you need shelter. Never, ever cook inside a tent. A well-ventilated vestibule or lobby area is fine and offers enough shelter. You can also use your tarpaulin to shelter an outdoor cooking area. Here are some more ideas:

• If you're car camping, then putting all your kitchen stuff in a plastic box is convenient. Later, the box can be upturned and used as a preparation area too.

• Keeping food cool is not so easy without a fridge. If you're backpacking, you can dunk whatever you need in a stream. Car campers can use a cool box and some sites will have a freezer so you can refreeze your ice packs. (See p132 for more tips on keeping food cool.)

• Folding tables and chairs are not obligatory and they have to be set up and kept clean. You could do without them, sit on the ground around the campfire, and eat just as happily.

Sealed bottles can be kept chilled naturally in cool rivers or streams

Dealing with large pests

Deterring insects is important (see pp106–7), but bigger pests can pose a real danger. Where in the world you are camping will determine which animals you may encounter, so do some pre-trip research into the wild animals that live in your destination of choice. Animals are attracted to your camp because they are attracted to your food, so always keep a tidy campsite, dispose of food and water properly, and keep your food safe. Any animal can carry disease, so if you do get bitten, seek medical attention.

Bears are an issue if you are camping in North America. They are also found in South America and some parts of Asia and Europe. They can run fast, and grizzlies can swim and climb trees. They also have an incredible sense of smell and are intelligent. The old trick of hanging your food stash from a tree has been abandoned in some US National Parks because the bears have learned to cut the rope to get the food. If you're camping where you may encounter bears, follow this basic code of practice:

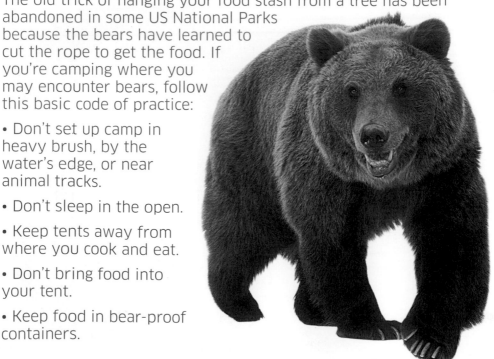

• Don't set up camp in heavy brush, by the water's edge, or near animal tracks.

• Don't sleep in the open.

• Keep tents away from where you cook and eat.

• Don't bring food into your tent.

• Keep food in bear-proof containers.

Bear attacks are very rare. But if you do encounter a grizzly, keep your group together, since bears are more intimidated by numbers, bang saucepans, and yell loudly. Don't trap the bear in any way; make sure it has a clear escape route.

Small mammals can be both bold and swift. If you notice any taking an interest in your camp, then make sure your food is safely stored away and don't leave rubbish around for creatures such as rats, mice, foxes, and raccoons to plunder. Skunks, found in North America, South America, and Asia, are nocturnal, and sometimes hang  around campsites in search of easy food. The viscous liquid they fire from glands near their anus stinks horribly, and can be fired over a distance of 3 metres (10ft), so stay clear. If you see a skunk round your campsite, avoid it. It may be rabid.

Snakes most often bite because the victim accidentally disturbed them. They are generally timid creatures and venomous ones will only bite you in self-defence. Familiarize yourself with the snake species you may encounter in your destination of choice and carry a snakebite kit if it's recommended for that location. But it's more useful to learn where you may find them, and use appropriate caution.

Collecting water

Because we grow up believing that we can only drink water that comes out of a tap or a bottle, it's easy for many of us to imagine that drinking water from a stream is fraught with danger. But in most situations, a simple purifying method should reassure you that your water is safe.

• When collecting water from a stream, choose a spot where it's flowing fast and clear.
• If you're taking water from a lake, avoid areas trampled by animals. Wade out if necessary.

There are several ways to purify water:

Boiling Although it's a bit inconvenient and wasteful of energy, boiling water for at least a minute will kill almost everything that might harm you. Boil water for longer at higher altitudes.

Water filters Pumping water by hand through a very fine filter removes bacteria and parasites, but not waterborne viruses.

Chemicals Essentially, this means adding either iodine or chlorine to water. The warmer the water the better they work, so colder water has to stand longer before it's safe to use. Chemicals add an unpleasant after-taste and don't always kill all pathogens, including the parasite that causes giardia.

Collect water from the clearest running source before purifying it.

Keeping camp

There's much more to camping than simply putting up your tent. Living outside is great fun, but it can also be a challenge at times. However, there are plenty of things you can do to make chores easier, and to ensure that your camping trip is a real holiday.

Camp living

Living in a tent is quite an education. You need to eat, wash up, keep clean, keep warm, and do all the stuff you do normally with all your mod cons – but without them. What's more, the focus of your "home life" will probably be quite different from living in a house. While it's possible to watch television when you're camping, it's rather missing the point. So with all those hours to fill without a screen to stare at, you'll find yourself reverting to the default position for humans – amusing each other. Here are some ideas to help:

• If there's a group of you, arrange your tents to create a circle or semi-circle, a kind of public area where you can meet and eat together.

• Sharing chores will bring you closer to your fellow campers and help to avoid arguments.

• Keeping things tidy and organised may not come naturally, but making the effort in a tent is worth it. Clothes left on your bedroom floor stay where they're put. Clothes on a tent floor can get wet.

• Try your best to keep dirt out of your tent and have a dustpan and brush handy.

• Leave your shoes or sandals at the tent door. If you like wandering around in bare feet, and keep a square of old carpet there to dry them on.

Nothing beats basking in the warmth of the campfire as the sun goes down.

Keeping dry

Rain can actually be one of the great pleasures of camping. Lying in a warm tent, inside a cosy sleeping bag, being lulled to sleep by the sound of raindrops on the flysheet is heavenly. However, that requires your tent and your sleeping bag to be dry.

The first commandment
If you're car camping, there's no reason why your sleeping bag should get wet in the first place, and if you're backpacking then it's almost the first commandment to keep your sleeping bag dry.

Test it first
The main thing to remember is that the time to find out that there is a weakness in your equipment or how you've used it is not when it's actually started raining. You don't have to be obsessive about it, but just checking on the condition of your tent as it ages, and how well it's pitched after a few days in one place is worth the trouble. If rain on a tent is romantic, rain in a tent is just plain depressing. Here are some tips:

• Keep the flysheet taut. This will stop it lying against the inner and allowing water to join you.

• Fix holes wherever they appear. Check the groundsheet periodically for punctures.

• Don't bring water into the tent with you, be that on your shoes or on your clothes. If you're soaked, then leave the wet clothes outside for now.

• Always make sure everyone has something dry and well-insulated to change into.

• If you're backpacking, then spare clothes are often limited to underwear. It's absolutely essential to keep your sleeping bag dry.

• In emergencies, you can dry a pair of socks inside your sleeping bag, and a damp thermal vest too.

• Keeping a tidy camp means that if it rains while you're out, your stuff won't get wet.

• Ponchos and umbrellas are handy for dashes to the lavatory. So, of course, are sandals.

Make your umbrella a sturdy one to withstand winds in exposed areas.

Keeping clean

Frankly, this is overrated. If you can't get a little grubby when you go camping, when can you? But if you're really determined to stay clean, then here are some tips:

• Many campsites have hot showers, but if not, there are solar-heated, portable showers on the market.

• Wild swimming is a great way to wash the dirt and sweat off, but don't overdo the detergent.

• Dirty clothes don't matter much, but underwear does. Wild laundry is possible on a warm day and trips to the laundrette are definitely allowed.

• Keeping hands clean is essential. Hand sanitizers are useful, especially with children around.

Toilet concerns

Perhaps the most common reason campers like to stay at campsites with facilities is that they want a flushing toilet. If you're wild camping though, you could dig a deep latrine, or use a chemical toilet (available from camping stores). If you're unable to squat, there are clever foldout cardboard toilet seats that can be recycled afterwards. If you are backpacking, dig a hole six inches deep and use that. Carry a lighter and burn the toilet paper. You have to unravel it a bit to get it flaming, but it will work.

Missing the odd bath doesn't matter, but a wash in pure water can be so refreshing.

Kitchen chores

The thought of doing chores without all the conveniences of modern life can put some people off camping altogether. But with some preparation, the everyday chores can be manageable, and even enjoyable. Children who won't stir themselves from the couch to clean up at home, often find it fun to help in the great outdoors. If you're backpacking, you'll also have the same old chores, but it's pleasant to find that you simply do everything in miniature.

• If you have access to a tap, use a water carrier so you don't have to make too many trips. But bear in mind that a litre of water weighs a kilogram (2.2lb).

• If there's no tap, then you'll have to rely on nearby streams, rivers, or lakes. Drinking water must be purified (see pp88–9) and young children should be supervised when collecting it.

• Washing up is less yucky if you've got gloves, a bowl, and some detergent handy. You can bring a tea-towel, but air drying works well outside.

• Every campsite has garbage on it. This is because no matter how careful people think they are, they always leave something. Make sure you dispose of your rubbish properly.

• Never bury food waste. Animals love a challenge. Burning cans after use gets rid of tempting residue.

Take old cutlery with you. Plastic will only end up in landfill sites.

Making a fire

Sitting around a fire with a group of friends or family is one of the great pleasures of camping. That's not surprising, because for our species, it's one of our oldest shared experiences. Fires are perfect for story-telling, toasting marshmallows, or just watching the flames. Not every campsite will let you light a fire, and others will have rules about what you can do and where you can do it. In the wild, you have to be very careful that your fire couldn't start a bigger one. Here are some ideas to consider:

• If you're permitted to light a fire at a campsite, then find out where it's allowed, and what the rules are.

• Some campsites only allow the use of a firepit or brazier.

• Many campsites have fire rings. These are patches of ground repeatedly used for fires, usually demarcated by stones. You should use them.

• If you're lighting a fire in woodland, clear leaves and other debris away first, until an area of bare earth is exposed.

• Only ever use fallen wood for fuel, and be sure you don't use more than you need.

• Don't light a fire which is overhung by anything else, like a tree, tent, or tarpaulin.

• Afterwards, make sure the fire is properly put out, using water if necessary, and bury the ashes with any top layer you've scraped off.

A tepee fire is the classic campfire, but be sure to build it in a safe place.

Types of fire

You can build a fire for two purposes, just for fun, or to cook a meal. For the latter, you'll need hearth stones or logs to prop a pan on, otherwise it's a question of what kind of fire you're going to build. First, you need three kinds of material to burn:

• **Tinder** can be bits of grass, or thin twigs, birch bark or even pine cones; anything dry and thin. Alternatively, you can use firelighters, or bits of newspaper.

• **Kindling** will be thicker twigs, and should be bone dry. Look out for dead twigs caught on branches, which will be drier still. Thick cardboard also works.

• **Firewood** should be thicker sticks and logs that will take a long time to burn through. If you're using a fire pit, you can use charcoal too.

Build your own

You don't have to build a recognised type of fire. You can just start with some small stuff and build it up from there. But here are four types of fire that bushcraft experts recommend.

The tepee Take a kindling branch, with some good twig stubs, drive it into the ground and arrange other sticks around it, propping them against the central stick to form a tepee shape. Leave a gap to push tinder or a firelighter in. This one produces heat and embers quickly so you could use it for cooking too.

The seminole Using the tepee technique, get a blaze going, and then add three or four chunky logs and slowly advance them into the embers from opposite angles, like a star. This is great for when you don't have much firewood, yet it will burn for some time.

The hunter's fire This is a really useful campfire to cook on because it catches rapidly and produces embers quickly. You can adapt it to burn longer if you also need it for warmth. (see pp104-5).

The lean-to Most useful in a wind, this gives warmth quickly and requires one green, live stick that is driven into the ground at an angle. The stick should be in line with the wind direction, with the buried end upwind. A line of dry sticks is then laid against the green one, forming a tunnel. This offers some protection while you introduce the tinder into the open end.

Building a fire

This hunter's fire is primarily designed to cook on, providing a lot of embers quickly, but it can also be adapted to last for warmth as well. The thicker logs either side are there to support a pan. If you want to sit by the fire at night, then use thicker kindling, or keep feeding it with more sticks to keep it going, you'll need plenty, but that's all just part of the fun.

1 First lay two thick logs parallel to each other. These can also be placed in a "v" shape. The idea is that they should be able to support your pan.

Lighting fires

There are several bushcraft methods for lighting a fire, but most campers would rather see the thing ablaze than struggle with a fire steel or magnifying glass. To light a fire easily, use a firelighter, or something like egg-boxes and paper, plus some twigs and dry grass as tinder and apply a match or lighter. Windproof lighters are a good idea if you camp in a windy area. Always have a back-up.

2 Start building layers of sticks between the logs. Each layer should be at right angles to the last. As the construction grows, you can place tinder in the central space.

3 You'll need four, five, or even six layers built on top of each other, depending on thickness and how many embers you need to cook on.

4 Once the stack is complete, you can light the tinder at the bottom. The space under the sticks will draw air in and fan the fire.

5 This kind of open kindling construction will burn fast. The logs on either side are supposed to catch fire, but if they're thick enough, they'll burn more slowly.

6 Once the stack has burned down, you can use the embers to cook over. If you need warmth or want to share the fire, you can add thicker logs later.

Building a fire **105**

Keeping the bugs off

There are millions of insect species. Inevitably, a few will do unpleasant things to you. The good news is that almost all bites and stings won't do any lasting damage, although there are exceptions. As always, prevention is better than cure but it's as well to know about the more harmful bugs.

Mosquitoes In some countries, mosquitoes carry the parasite that causes malaria. If you are camping in a country you don't know, check the status of mosquito-borne diseases there and seek medical advice ahead of time.

Ticks These pinhead-sized creatures have powerful jaws that lock on to you so the tick can suck your blood. After a day or so they can swell to the size of a pea. Ticks carry bacteria, which cause Lyme's Disease, which is treatable by antibiotics, but nasty if left undiagnosed. If you are bitten by a tick, grip the insect firmly as near as possible to its jaws and pull it off. Put it in a container for possible later testing. If a rash develops around the bite between three days and a month later, get medical advice.

Some advice on repellents:

• Many people use an insect repellent based on DEET, developed by the US military for jungle warfare. It can't be used by very young children or on broken skin, however. It is also a solvent, and since much outdoor equipment is made of petrochemical-based fibres, your clothing can be degraded by it.

• Citronella oil is an effective alternative to DEET, but it has to be used more frequently.

• Two tried and tested alternatives are Odomos cream, an ayurvedic insect repellent, and Avon's Skin So Soft body spray. This isn't manufactured as a repellent, but stops midges.

• Clothing impregnated with repellents work well but the effect wears off with washing.

• If you suffer an allergy to stings, don't forget to carry your medication.

First aid

It's the big disasters we worry about, from breaking a leg to getting struck by lightning. But in reality it's the small mishaps that most often bother us, from scratches and sprains, to rashes and sunburn. See right for some of the most common camping ailments, and what to do about them.

You should really aim to be self-sufficient for most kinds of problems, and have a first-aid kit that allows you to be so. If you're backpacking, then medical attention for more serious injuries isn't readily available. Further research into wilderness medicine is highly recommended.

Invest in a properly equipped first aid kit to help you deal with the most common accidents.

Blisters are caused when skin is rubbed repeatedly against a surface, like the inside of a boot. Make sure yours fit well and use hiking socks. If you feel a blister forming, then stop and inspect the affected area. If a blister has formed, drain it with a needle prick and use gel-like dressings to protect it.

Bruises are common after a fall. If the injury is sufficiently painful, apply something cold to the affected area, like a cold wet cloth.

Cramp is often caused by dehydration, which can lead to more serious heat exhaustion. Relieve pain by flexing the affected muscle. In hot weather, use rehydration salts, or eat salted nuts. Dehydration can be exacerbated by altitude.

Grazes must have all the dirt and grit washed out of them with clean water and an antiseptic cream applied. Deeper cuts will need dressing.

Sunburn is much worse at altitudes, but wherever you are, keep applying protective suncream.

Plant stings and burns can be nasty. Learn to recognise plants with the toxic chemical urushiol and avoid them. Wash stings and burns with cold water and apply either camomile lotion, or for more serious cases, hydrocortisone cream.

Wild swimming

One of the great pleasures of life outdoors is the opportunity to swim in some truly memorable places. Whether it's an early morning dip after spending the night on a beach, or diving into a mountain lake after a hard day's walking, swimming outside adds lustre to any adventure. But before you jump in, here are some ideas to bear in mind:

• Wild swimming is only dangerous if you're reckless about it. Take some time to research and understand local conditions, tides, and undercurrents.

• Don't swim more than 100 metres (300ft) offshore without some kind of escort.

• If you haven't often swum outdoors, build up slowly. It might seem a great idea to cross a river or lake, but it's not so much fun when you're halfway across and running out of energy.

• If the water is really cold, exhale on entry. It's a neat way to avoid the hyperventilation that follows when your chest contracts on contact with the water.

• If you're going to skinny dip, make sure that you do so with tact and consideration.

Taking a dip can be exhilarating, but watch out for strong currents.

Food for free

Surviving on food you can find growing wild isn't easy; it takes considerable expertise. But you can do it in a small way. You'll be familiar with blueberries, raspberries, blackberries, and wild strawberries, but you won't have seen many white berries in a shop, because they're almost all poisonous, so avoid them. Mushrooms too can be deceptive, so don't touch them, or learn from an expert. While hunting isn't an option for most of us, fishing certainly is. Fresh trout baked in your campfire embers tastes divine, and wild thyme, garlic, or wood sorrel add wonderful flavours. But consider these points:

• Only eat what you can identify for sure.

• Think about habitats. Field mushrooms grow in fields, so mushrooms that look like field mushrooms but are growing in woods could be Death Caps.

• There may be local rules or permit requirements for hunting and fishing, so check first.

• Mint tea made from fresh mint leaves is the best there is. But as a general rule, don't pick more than you need. The plant needs to survive too.

Pack a fishing rod and you may be lucky enough to catch your own supper.

Reading the weather

Living outdoors, the weather becomes more important in our lives. Learning to read the weather is a useful art, although it shouldn't stop you taking note of a professional forecast. But more than that, it's enriching to have a feel for what the atmosphere is doing. Wind, cloud, humidity, and temperature are in constant flux around the planet. A little basic research will help you predict the weather where you are.

Signs of good weather

Cirrus are thin, wispy clouds above 20,000ft formed of ice crystals. Their shape follows the direction of air movement and they generally indicate good weather.

Cumulus are the beautiful, puffy white clouds, formed by convection as warm moist air rises on a summer's day. Although they can also form into something less benign.

Altocumulus form at a higher altitude than cumulus clouds, and create a "mackerel" sky, indicating fair weather. In summer they can presage a thunderstorm.

Signs of bad weather

Cumulonimbus are the thunderstorm clouds whose base is near the ground but which rise through the sky, forming distinctive anvil-heads. As they grow, they become unstable, and generate static electricity.

Altostratus form as a large mass of air lifts and condenses, these clouds usually develop below 20,000ft, can produce precipitation and indicate a new weather front bringing more rain or snow.

Cirrostratus are sheets of high-altitude cloud formed by ice crystals. They can be thousands of feet thick, and yet almost transparent. Sometimes they form a halo around the sun or moon.

Nimbostratus are the thick, grey clouds common in temperate regions. These dense rain clouds form below 10,000ft.

Stargazing

One of the paradoxes of modern life is that the more we know about the universe, the less most of us can see of it, thanks to light pollution. So camping can be a great opportunity to reconnect with the night sky.

The changing sky

What you see varies depending on both the time of year and the time of night. And while the stars appear in the same places from year to year, the positions of the moon and planets are constantly changing. Unless you are close to the equator, the constellations around the celestial poles will always remain above the horizon as the Earth rotates, and are known as circumpolar. Computer programs can now predict the night sky at any given time and date, but while camping you can also use a chart called a planisphere.

Adapting to the dark

At night, your eyes become much more sensitive, but this "dark adaptation" builds slowly. Allow ten minutes for your eyes to adjust before you start, and to preserve your night vision, use a flashlight with a red filter. You don't need specialist equipment, just a good novice's introduction to astronomy. Binoculars will reveal extra detail on the moon, and highlight other notable planets, but a pair of naked eyes will suffice.

The Milky Way is spectacular in the clear night sky

What you may see

What you see in the night sky will of course depend upon where in the world you are looking from. Some stars, and planets such as red Mars, Venus, Saturn, and Jupiter will be visible from north and south of the equator, but both the northern and southern hemispheres have their own constellations, particularly around the poles.

Finding the northern polestar

In the northern hemisphere, knowing the location of the polestar is the first step in orientating yourself. It's less than one degree off the north pole, and although it's not the brightest star, it stays put over the Earth's axis. Find the constellation of Ursa Major (see right), find its two pointers, and extend the distance between them five times to arrive near the polestar, the brightest star in the constellation of Ursa Minor.

Finding the south celestial pole

In the southern sky, although the famous Southern Cross is not the most striking feature, its regular, diamond-like shape is easy to identify, and acts as a pointer to the celestial pole. Extend the long axis of the Cross fivefold to reach the southern pole, an area bereft of any stars of note. As a further rough guide, the south celestial pole forms a triangle with the bright stars Canopus and Achernar.

The two stars at the end of Ursa Major will point you to the polestar.

Map-reading skills

Humans are used to orientating themselves and we do it in all kinds of ways, from following street signs to asking directions. Nothing, however, compares to reading a good map. Develop map-reading skills, and not only will you be able to figure out where you are and where to go without needing signs or advice, but you'll also understand a lot more about the geography and history of the place you're visiting.

Find your way out of trouble with a topographic map. Unlike tourist maps, topographic ones are much more detailed, showing the location of forests and water. Contour lines show whether the ground is steep or flat, and will even tell you the altitude you might reach. Marked footpaths can also indicate your legal status on a piece of land, while the map's scale will allow you to judge distance. Put the skill of map reading with the ability to use a compass, and you'll be able to orientate yourself in the middle of nowhere.

Keep your map in a waterproof bag so you can use it in any weather.

Some pointers to exploring the outdoors:

Before you set out, fold the map so that it shows the relevant area, and orientate it in your map case so the direction you're heading in appears at the top. You'll find it easier to follow.

Maps are made of paper, and get soggy when wet. Use a map case or buy a laminated or plastic map.

Maps can show the kind of terrain you will cross on a walk. Learn to calibrate the information on the map to what you experience.

Judge how much ascent is involved in your walk. A lot of uphill walking can add greatly to the time and effort involved.

When high up, take some time to study how the sweep of landscape in front of you matches the topographic information on the map.

With a compass you can orientate yourself even if you don't have a map.

Wet weather inspiration

Sooner or later it will rain when you're camping. Far from being the end of the world, this is actually a great opportunity to relax, hang out, talk, and reflect. If you've sorted your gear out correctly, it's going to take a biblical flood to drown out the fun. And while you're waiting for the sun to come out, here are some ideas:

• It might be raining, but is it cold? Summer showers aren't that bad once you get outside into them. Put on your raingear and go for a walk.

• Surfing is the ideal wet-weather activity. Swimming in the rain is almost as good. You're going to get wet anyway, so why not go all the way?

• Find a laundrette and do your washing.

• Stay in bed. Dozing, listening to the rain pattering on the flysheet, and waiting for the kettle to boil can be a blissful scene.

• Observe the three-day law. After three days of nothing but rain, you qualify for a hotel room – or else just head home.

There really can be a rainbow of opportunity among the dark clouds.

Fun things to do

The real joy of camping is not just about putting up tents and cooking on a fire. Living outside is a transformatory experience, and a healthy one too. You'll sleep better, assuming your bed is comfortable, and you'll lose weight. Most of all you'll have the chance to do a whole range of fun things you may never have tried before. Saving money by camping means there may be funds left over to try an outdoor sport you've always fancied, anything from rock climbing to white-water rafting. Backpacking is a way to understand a landscape more fully than you ever have before. Mostly, camping is a way to slow down, and take some time to look around. Here are some other fun things to do:

- Bird watching
- Identifying flowers or insects
- Fishing
- Hide and seek
- Kite flying
- Ball games
- Photography
- Stories round the campfire
- Tracking animals
- Treasure hunts
- Tree climbing
- Yoga

Kick a ball around together on the beach. Inexpensive, good clean fun.

Camp cooking

How much equipment you take with you to cook
your food will depend on the type of campsite
(or wilderness) that you choose, and whether you are
travelling light, or transporting everything by car.
So you can take a simple Trangia stove with its
integrated pots and pans, or a more sophisticated set
of culinary tools. And unless you're travelling really
light, it's worth taking a few basic ingredients with
you too. See the next few pages for some useful
suggestions for what to take and how to store it.

Kitchen essentials

Make your camp kitchen as simple or as sophisticated as you wish, and use this collection of equipment as your guide. It's a basic list that will enable you to cook the delicious recipes that follow, but you can add to it, or leave behind whatever you like.

Camp cooking kit
If you are doing anything other than backpacking, these are your essentials for producing hot food and drinks, and will allow you to cook a surprisingly wide variety of dishes.

stove plus gas/matches. (Keep boxes of matches in an airtight container such as a jar with a lid)

2 pans with lids, ideally non-stick (easier to wash up)

kettle

1 large frying pan or wok, (use non-stick if possible)

Camp cutlery and crockery
Pack non-breakable items and at least 1 per person of the following:

Mugs, Large **plates** with rims, **Bowls**, **Knives, Forks, Spoons, Teaspoons, Tumblers**

Camp kitchen drawer

As well as the following, you'll need: a large **cool box** and **freezer packs**, **water container**, **can opener**, clean **glass jar** with lid (for mixing marinades and dressings), **foil** (for creating parcels to bake in the campfire, covering saucepans, and cooked food).

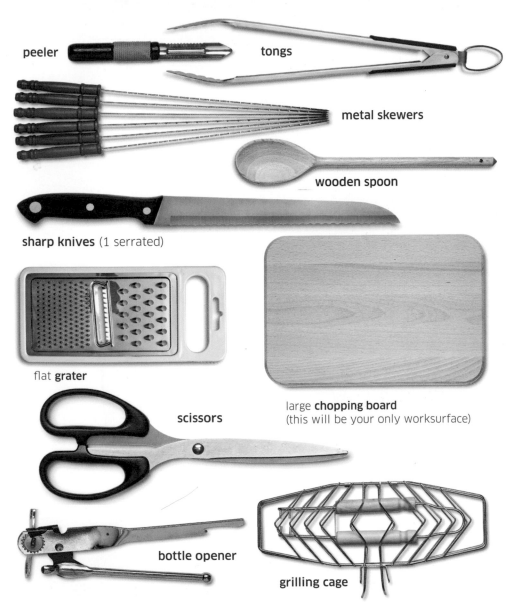

peeler

tongs

metal skewers

wooden spoon

sharp knives (1 serrated)

flat **grater**

scissors

large **chopping board**
(this will be your only worksurface)

bottle opener

grilling cage

Larder essentials

For camp kitchen comfort, you'll need to take a mini larder with you, stocked with the ingredients that you commonly use. But bear in mind, your choice of stockcupboard goodies must be camping-conscious.

Make it tasty It's worth taking a few strongly flavoured ingredients along, as they will instantly add piquancy to the simplest food. You can easily mix quick marinades and glazes by putting the ingredients in a clean glass jar, securing it with a lid, and giving it a good shake to combine. Even the most basic combination of oil, herbs, and balsamic vinegar will add variety to anything you grill over the campfire.

Make it fast You may be fortunate enough to have a convenient supply of fresh fruit and vegetables where you camp, but if not, cans and jars of preserved food are really useful. Remember, too, that being outside will sharpen everyone's appetite, so try to choose dishes that are quick to cook, or that everyone can help to prepare and cook – that way you're sure to be happy campers.

Make it simple Pack these basics in a small box and you'll be equipped for anything. To cut down on weight and bulk, you can discard the original packaging and transfer what you need for your trip into food bags that are lighter and easier to transport:

salt and pepper (in airtight containers to keep dry), mixed **herbs**, **olive oil**, **sunflower oil**, tube of **garlic purée**, tube of **mustard**, tube of **tomato purée**, **balsamic vinegar** (in a small spray-type bottle for grilling and making dressings), **stock cubes**, **Tabasco** sauce, **lemon juice** (bottled is fine), canned **fish**, canned **tomatoes**, **jars of antipasti** – grilled **aubergines**, **artichokes**, **peppers**, or **sun-dried tomatoes**, small jar of **curry paste** or **curry powder**, cans or cartons of UHT **coconut milk**, UHT **milk**, UHT **soured cream**, **Parmesan cheese**, **rice**, **noodles**, **couscous**, snack packs of "ready to eat" **apricots**, ground **cinnamon**, runny **honey**, **maple syrup**, **eggs**, **pancake mix**.

Salt and pepper are vital companions for spicing up your meals. Get some lightweight, mini-cruets for easy transportation.

Keeping food cold

Keeping raw food properly chilled is vital when camping. If meat, poultry, fish, or dairy products get warm before they are cooked, there is a serious risk of food poisoning. On a campsite with full facilities, you may have access to a refrigerator, but most campers will have to pack a cool box.

Use ice packs Use several frozen packs in your ice box to keep the temperature as low as possible. Remember to refreeze them daily.

Do the "frozen milk" trick Freeze a carton of milk before you leave on Friday evening and store it at the bottom of your cool box. It will de-frost nicely over the weekend, providing you with cold milk for your cereal on Sunday morning. In the meantime it acts as an ice block, keeping your cool box cold.

Buy a bag of ice Supermarkets sell ice bags and your fishmonger may give you ice if you buy their fish.

Use the river Great for cooling bottles, but put tightly sealed bottles and cartons in a net bag and 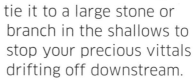 tie it to a large stone or branch in the shallows to stop your precious vittals drifting off downstream.

Ice packs in your cool box will keep your food chilled for several days.

Keeping food hot

Once you have reheated or cooked your food, you'll want it to stay hot until you serve it – particularly important if you have to cook several items on just one or two camp stove rings. But with a few simple tips, you can ensure everyone enjoys a hot meal.

Insulate with cloths and newspaper To keep pans of food hot for a good 20 minutes, place the covered pan on newspaper and throw a towel over to insulate.

Add some sauce Once served, boiled vegetables can go cold very quickly, so try serving them in a hot sauce – it will add flavour too.

Make a "hot" box A cool box can be used as a hot box, just as a thermos flask can keep milk cold or hot. Fill a cool box with warm air from the fire, put the pan inside, and seal the box.

Use a flask If you need to keep a sauce hot while you cook other ingredients, pour it into a flask and seal.

Round 'em up Get everyone rounded up, and ready to eat before serving, to avoid anyone getting a cold meal.

Flasks are friends to hot drinks, soups, and sauces. Seal them tightly for best results.

Recipes

Have you noticed how everything tastes better when eaten outside? Cooking and eating in the fresh air is one of the best things about camping, whether it's frying up a hearty breakfast over the camp stove, baking a fish (that you've caught yourself) in the campfire embers, or just reheating a pot of stew. Here are some irresistible recipes for the camp stove and fire, as well as some home-cooked comforts to make and take with you.

Look for these symbols: Cook on the campfire   Cook in a frying pan   Cook in a saucepan

Camp stove cooking

These recipes have been created and tested by genuine campers who know what works on a camp stove. Many of them are one-pot meals and can easily be cooked on a single ring burner. Look for the pan symbols with each recipe which will tell you whether you will need one or two pots to cook it. Whether you use a single, double, or triple burner, cooking on a camp stove is not difficult, but there are a few essential safety issues that you should be aware of.

The most important rule is that you should NEVER cook inside a tent because of the risk of fire. Set up the stove a little distance away, or if you need shelter, put up a tarpaulin. An attached wind guard can be really useful if you're cooking in bad weather, but always take care near dry wood and grass. Make sure you know how to turn the gas off and that you can reach the valve at all times.

Keep things simple and try not to create too much washing up. Give everyone a fork and eat out of the pan if you're feeling really lazy. Perhaps most importantly though, make those portions extra generous – spending so much time outside makes people really hungry, so cook even more than you would at home – and have fun!

Breakfast medley

A great way to kick-start the day, cook this in a large non-stick frying pan on the stove or campfire

SERVES **4**
TIME TO COOK **20 MINS**

a little butter or oil for frying

8 sausages

4 rashers of bacon, chopped

handful of button mushrooms

handful of cherry tomatoes

4 eggs, beaten

1 Fry the sausages for 10–15 minutes then add the bacon, and fry until the bacon starts to crisp.

2 Now add the mushrooms and tomatoes until they begin to soften.

3 Remove all the ingredients from the pan for a few moments.

4 Add a little more butter or oil to the pan and once hot, pour in the eggs.

5 After a minute add the sausages, bacon, mushrooms, and tomatoes, pressing them down into the egg, and cook gently until the top sets.

6 Turn out onto a plate and serve with crusty bread or fresh toast.

If you don't eat meat, you could use vegetarian sausages instead, and fry some tiny cubed potato with the mushrooms and tomatoes

Spanish omelette

Add any other vegetables you like to this classic recipe

SERVES **4**

TIME TO COOK **10 MINS**

8 eggs

salt and pepper

mixed dried herbs

1 tbsp butter

1 onion, finely chopped

1 pepper, finely chopped

2 cooked potatoes, diced into 1cm (½in) pieces

2 cooked carrots, diced into 1cm (½in) pieces

1 Beat the eggs with the salt and pepper and mixed herbs.

2 In a non-stick frying pan fry the onion and pepper in the butter until they begin to soften, then add the other vegetables. Cook for a further minute, then add the eggs. Leave to cook on a very gentle heat with the lid on until the egg is firm on the top.

3 Turn the omelette out onto a plate so that the brown top is uppermost and cut into quarters.

You could use canned vegetables for this omelette, but drain them first

Chillied eggs

A quick supper, or even breakfast dish, the chilli adds a great kick

SERVES **4**
TIME TO COOK **15 MINS**

1 large onion, finely chopped

1 green pepper, finely chopped

1 tbsp oil

2 garlic cloves, crushed or 1 tsp garlic purée

1–2 tsp of chilli powder or 1–2 tsp of tabasco sauce

2 400g (14oz) cans chopped tomatoes

4 free-range eggs

4 tbsp of cheese, grated

handful fresh parsley, chopped

1 Fry the onions and pepper in oil until soft, then add the garlic and chilli.

2 Pour in the tomatoes and simmer with the lid off for 10 mins. Make "holes" in the tomato sauce and break the eggs into these. Cover the pan and cook gently for 5 minutes until the eggs are cooked. Spread with cheese and cook for a further few minutes with the lid on until the cheese melts.

3 Sprinkle plenty of chopped parsley over and serve with rice, potatoes or crusty bread.

Sausage and bean hotpot

Use any kind of sausages and canned beans in this one-pot meal

SERVES **4**

TIME TO COOK **25 MINS**

8 or 12 good quality sausages

1 tbsp oil

1 400g (14oz) can cannellini beans

1 400g (14oz) can flageolet beans

¼ tsp dried chilli flakes or ½ tsp tabasco sauce

2 large tsp mustard

2 400g (14oz) cans chopped tomatoes

salt and pepper

handful of fresh parsley, chopped

1 Fry the sausages in oil for approximately 20 minutes until cooked. Remove from the pan and keep warm.

2 Drain the cannellini and flageolet beans and add to the pan with the chilli, mustard, and tomatoes (with their juice) and heat through.

3 Cut the cooked sausages in half lengthways, and add to tomato and bean sauce. Season and stir the parsley through.

3 Serve with bread or rice.

Beef stroganoff with noodles

A ten-minute supper dish to serve with buttered pasta

SERVES **4**

TIME TO COOK **10 MINS**

2 large onions, finely chopped

2 or 3 large handfuls mushrooms, sliced

1 tbsp oil

1 tbsp butter

500g beef (rump or fillet), thinly sliced into strips

1 large tub soured cream

500g (1lb 2oz) pack dried pasta

salt and pepper

handful of fresh parsley, chopped

1 Fry the onions and mushrooms in the oil and butter for a few minutes, then add the beef and continue cooking for a further few minutes.

2 Mix in the soured cream and season well. Keep warm while you cook the pasta according to the instructions on the packet.

3 Add a little more butter to the pasta and then serve with the stroganoff and parsley sprinkled over.

Meatballs with vegetable noodles

Here the liver pâté is a great shortcut to rich flavour and nutrients

SERVES **4**
TIME TO COOK **30 MINS**

For the sauce:
1 onion, finely chopped

1 small pepper, finely chopped

2 tbs oil

2 garlic cloves, crushed, or 1 tsp garlic purée

½ tsp mixed herbs

1 400g (14oz) can chopped tomatoes

1 tub crème fraîche (or alternative)

For the meatballs:
500g (1lb 2oz) minced beef

1 tub chicken liver pâté (or other)

1 onion, very finely chopped

½ tsp mixed herbs

salt and pepper

to serve, 4 "nests" of noodles

1 To make the sauce; fry the onion and pepper in oil with garlic and herbs, add the tomatoes, and simmer for about 10 minutes.

2 Add the crème fraîche and season. Keep warm.

3 To make the meatballs, mix all the ingredients in a bowl and form into ping-pong sized balls. Using a frying pan or wok, fry them in batches for approximately 10 minutes and add to the vegetable sauce as they cook.

4 Cook the meatballs and sauce for a further 10 minutes.

5 Boil the noodles according to instructions on packet, drain and stir into meatballs mixture and serve.

Turkish lamb couscous

Requiring only hot stock, couscous is the perfect camp food

SERVES **4**

TIME TO COOK **20 MINS**

1 large onion, roughly chopped

500g (1lb 2oz) of minced lamb

1 tbsp olive oil

1 100g (3½oz) "snack pack" of ready to eat apricots and/or raisins, roughly chopped

100g (3½oz) of pine nuts

1 tsp ground cinnamon

2 mugs couscous

1 stock cube

salt and pepper

1 Fry the onion and lamb in the olive oil for a few minutes, breaking up the mince as it cooks.

2 Add the chopped fruit, pine nuts and cinnamon and keep warm.

3 Put the couscous in a bowl and cover with boiling water. Crumble in a stock cube and stir to dissolve evenly. Set aside for 5 minutes and then add to the lamb mixture.

4 Simmer with a lid on for 5-10 minutes, adding a little more water if necessary. Season and fork in some more oil before serving.

Mediterranean vegetable couscous

A quick to cook dish that needs no fresh ingredients

SERVES **4**
TIME TO COOK **15 MINS**

1 vegetable stock cube

2 mugs couscous

1 jar sun dried tomatoes in oil, drained and roughly chopped

1 jar sweet red peppers in oil, drained and sliced

1 jar artichokes in oil, drained and roughly chopped

salt and pepper

juice of 1 lemon

dried chilli flakes

1 Dissolve the stock cube in 1½ mugs of boiling water. Add the couscous and leave, keeping warm for 10 minutes. Once all the water has been absorbed, add the chopped drained vegetables to the couscous.

2 Gently heat the couscous and vegetables through in a pan and use a fork to mix the seasoning, lemon juice, and chilli flakes in.

2 Serve with slices of chorizo sausage.

Easy vegetable curry

Canned vegetables can replace fresh ones in this quick recipe

SERVES **4**
TIME TO COOK **10 MINS**

2 onions, roughly chopped

2 carrots, sliced

2 courgettes or 2 peppers or 2 tomatoes (or a mix of all 3) sliced

2 tbsp oil

2 tbsp curry paste

1 400g (14oz) can chickpeas, drained

1 400ml (14fl oz) carton or can coconut milk

1 Fry the onions, carrots, courgettes, peppers, and tomatoes or other fresh vegetables in the oil until soft.

2 Add the curry paste, chickpeas, and coconut milk and bring to the boil, then simmer for 5 minutes.

3 Serve with boiled rice or naan.

Serve this simple, creamy curry with a spoonful of spicy mango, or lime pickle

Mushroom risotto

Cook arborio rice if you can, but if not, any long-grain type will do

SERVES **4**
TIME TO COOK **20 MINS**

1 onion, finely chopped

2 tbsp olive oil

2 mugs of rice

1 can beef consommé plus
enough water to make 4 mugs
of hot stock (or a dissolved
stock cube with the same
amount of liquid)

2 jars or cans of mixed
mushrooms, drained

1 small tub of dried
Parmesan cheese

salt and pepper

1 Fry the onion in the olive oil until softened, then add the rice, stir and coat the rice, then gradually add the 4 mugs of consommé or stock.

2 Cover with a lid and simmer until the rice is cooked and the liquid has been absorbed, adding a little more water if required.

3 Stir in the mushrooms and Parmesan cheese, and season to taste. Heat all the way through and serve.

White wine or vegetable stock can replace the consommé

Tuna and parsley with pasta

A super-fast, cheap, and fresh-tasting pasta sauce

SERVES **4**
TIME TO COOK **5 MINS**

2 cloves of garlic, crushed, or 1 tsp garlic purée

large bunch of fresh parsley, finely chopped

2 tbsp olive oil

2 cans tuna, drained

juice of 2 small lemons

½ 500g pack of pasta shells

1 small tub of dried Parmesan cheese

salt and pepper

1 Fry the garlic and parsley in the oil for a few minutes. Add the tuna and lemon juice and keep warm while you cook the pasta according to the instructions on the packet.

2 Drain and add the tuna and parsley mixture, along with the Parmesan cheese and seasoning.

3 Stir through, adding a little more oil if you wish, and serve.

Puttanesca

A colourful, vividly flavoured sauce to go with any dried pasta

SERVES **4**
TIME TO COOK **5 MINS**

2 cloves of garlic, crushed, or 1 tsp garlic purée

2 tbps olive oil

2 400g (14oz) cans tomatoes, chopped

½ tsp chilli flakes

½ small jar capers

1 jar pitted black olives, drained

2 tins anchovies in oil, drained

500g (1lb 2oz) pack dried spaghetti or other pasta

Parmesan cheese, grated

1 Gently fry the garlic in the olive oil, then add the tomatoes, chilli flakes, capers, olives, and anchovies. Simmer gently for 5 minutes.

2 Keep the sauce warm while you cook the spaghetti or other pasta according to pack instructions.

3 Drain the spaghetti or other pasta and toss the sauce through it.

4 Serve with grated Parmesan cheese.

With plenty of garlic and a little kick of chilli, this pasta sauce will keep campers warm from the inside out

Ratatouille

This quick and extravagant "holiday" version is made in minutes

SERVES **4**

TIME TO COOK **5 MINS**

1 large onion, chopped

1 tbsp olive oil

2 cloves of garlic, crushed, or 1 tsp garlic purée

1 jar of peppers in oil, drained and sliced

1 jar of courgettes in oil, drained and sliced

1 pot of ready prepared aubergines in oil, drained

1 400g (14oz) can chopped tomatoes

salt and pepper

handful grated cheese

chorizo sausage, sliced (optional)

1 Fry the onion in the olive oil until soft and add the garlic.

2 Add the peppers, courgettes, and aubergines. Now add the tomatoes, season and simmer for a few minutes.

3 Scatter the cheese over and serve with sliced chorizo sausage if desired.

You can cook this with fresh aubergine, courgettes, and peppers instead; just fry them with the onions

Prawns with noodles

If using frozen prawns, add another five minutes cooking time

SERVES **4**

TIME TO COOK **5 MINS**

1 onion, chopped

1 pepper, sliced

1 tbsp oil

pinch dried chilli flakes

2 cloves garlic, crushed or ½ tsp garlic purée

250g (9oz) tiger/king prawns

soy sauce

1 200ml (7fl oz) can (or carton) coconut milk

1 200ml (7fl oz) can bean sprouts, drained

4 "nests" egg or rice noodles

large handful coriander, roughly chopped

1 Fry the onion and pepper in oil. Add chilli and garlic and gently fry for a few more minutes.

2 Add the prawns and stir fry until they begin to colour, add a few drops of soy sauce then add the coconut milk and bean sprouts. Bring to the boil and keep warm.

3 Cook the noodles according to instructions on packet, drain and add to prawn mix.

4 Season the prawns and add the coriander just before serving them ladled over the noodles.

For a vegetarian meal, substitute the prawns with chopped mushrooms or another vegetable

Sea bass with potatoes and tomatoes

This simple, layered dish is the perfect one-pan meal

SERVES **4**

TIME TO COOK **20 MINS**

2 tbsp olive oil

1 large red onion, finely sliced

4 potatoes, peeled and finely sliced

4 tomatoes, sliced

4 small fillets of sea bass

juice of 1 lemon

1 large glass white wine

½ jar of capers (optional)

salt and pepper

1 Start by pouring the oil into the pan and then add a layer of the onions followed by the potatoes, then the tomatoes and finally put the fish on top. Sprinkle with the lemon juice, wine, and capers (if using) and season.

2 Cook, covered with a lid over a low heat for about 20 minutes until the fish is cooked and the flesh is no longer translucent. (You could also use any white fish steaks, but increase the cooking time by 5 minutes as they will be thicker than fillets).

You could make dish with any white fish fillets such as sea bream, plaice, sole, mullet or tilapia

Fish soup

This is an incredibly easy one-pot meal that can be made with any fresh or even smoked fish you have available

SERVES **4**

TIME TO COOK **20 MINS**

500g (1lb 2oz) white fish, all bones removed and chopped

handful button mushrooms, sliced

handful parsley, chopped

handful dill, chopped

1 400g (14oz) can chopped tomatoes

1 mug of dry cider

2 tbsp calvados (optional but very warming/recommended)

1 mug of fish stock (or vegetable stock will do)

salt and pepper

1 Put all the ingredients in a large pan and simmer gently, largely undisturbed, for 20 minutes.

2 Season the soup and serve with some crusty bread.

Add some small cubes of potato to turn this soup into a hearty meal

Sweet apple omelette

This is an easy family favourite that can be made with one, or a combination of such fruits as apples, pears, plums, or bananas

SERVES **4**

TIME TO COOK **20 MINS**

4 free-range eggs

1 small squeezy tube condensed milk

2 eating apples

2 tbsp butter

brandy (optional)

1 Beat the eggs with approximately 4 tablespoons of condensed milk.

2 Slice the apples and fry gently in the butter until soft.

3 Add the egg mixture and once set, flip over in the pan. Drizzle with brandy, if desired, and serve.

Make great French toast by soaking slices of bread in the egg and condensed milk, then frying in butter

Banana fritters

Syrupy and indulgent, these are made with easy to find ingredients

SERVES **4**
TIME TO COOK **5 MINS**

packet of pancake mix
plus eggs

1-2 tbsp butter for frying

1 banana (per person) sliced
lengthways

maple syrup or runny honey

1 Make up the pancake batter with eggs and water according to the instructions on the packet, but only use ⅓–½ of the amount of water specified. The consistency should be like thick paint.

2 Heat a knob of butter, the size of a walnut, in a frying pan. Dip the banana slices in the batter and fry in the hot butter until they are golden brown on both sides.

3 Serve hot with maple syrup or runny honey dribbled over them.

These fritters could be made with sliced and cored apples, and pears and pineapple rings work well, too

Campfire cooking

Cooking and eating together around a campfire or barbecue is one of the greatest pleasures of a camping trip. The recipes in this section are simple and quick to make, but pack plenty of flavour. Follow these few simple guidelines to ensure that what you serve is edible.

Light the campfire or barbecue in plenty of time before you begin cooking so that the fire embers or barbecue coals have turned white before you start – never grill over leaping flames. Most of these recipes include marinades that would normally be left to coat the meat for several hours in a refrigerator, but this is obviously impractical when you are cooking outdoors. So instead, the recipes suggest marinating for just 20 minutes in a chilled cool box.

Remember to discard any unused marinade, and not to pour it over cooked food. Do check that chicken, pork, and fish is cooked through, but lamb and beef will actually be more tender if you cook it so that it's still slightly pink.

Whole fish in foil baked in embers

A simple way to cook whole fish that seals in all the flavours

SERVES **4**

TIME TO COOK **14 MINS**

4 whole trout or 1 (or 2 large salmon to serve 4), cleaned and gutted

1 tbsp of butter

2 lemons, sliced

handful of herbs (thyme, oregano, basil, parsley, or a mix of your choice

salt and pepper

2 tbsp olive oil

1 Inside the cavity of each fish put a small knob of butter, some lemon slices and a few of the herbs. Season with salt and pepper. Now rub each fish in olive oil to prevent it sticking to the foil and wrap in a generous parcel of 2 or 3 layers of foil. Make sure that it is completely sealed so that the juices do not leak out.

2 Carefully place the foil parcels in the glowing embers of the fire (you will need a set of tongs). You do not have to completely cover the packages, just nestle them into the ashes. You would normally allow 15–20 minutes to cook the fish in an oven, but the heat will be more intense in the fire, so check the fish after 12–14 minutes.

This is the most delicious and satisfying way to cook fish that you have caught yourself

Vegetables parcels baked in embers

These different fillings use the same method. Try these suggestions or experiment with your own combinations

SERVES **4**
TIME TO COOK **30 MINS**

Sweet potato, green beans, and bacon

2 sweet potatoes peeled and chopped into 2.5cm (1in) cubes

4 tbsp olive oil

8 sage leaves, torn

handful of fine green beans, topped and tailed

6 rashers smoked streaky bacon, cut into 2.5cm (1in) chunks

salt and pepper

3-4 tbsp water

Ratatouille style

1 aubergine, chopped into 2.5cm (1in) cubes

3 courgettes chopped into 2.5cm (1in) cubes

1 red, orange or green pepper cut into 2.5cm (1in) pieces

1 onion, chopped

2 cloves of garlic, crushed

2 large tomatoes, cut into 2.5cm (1in) pieces

2 tbsp fresh oregano, chopped

salt and pepper

3-4 tbsp water

1 Combine all the ingredients in a bowl and then tear 4 generous sheets of foil, laying them on top of one another. Put all the ingredients in the centre, add the water, and carefully seal each layer of foil, one after another. Make sure that it is folded over and completely sealed so that the juices do not leak out.

2 Carefully place the foil parcels in the glowing embers of the fire (you will need a set of tongs). You do not have to completely cover the packages, just nestle them into the ashes.

3 Leave the sweet potato or ratatouille-style parcels to cook for 20-30 minutes, then open and serve.

Swordfish skewers with green salsa

Choose firm-fleshed fish for the barbecue or campfire so it holds together. It should cook quickly but remain moist and tender

SERVES **4**

TIME TO COOK **8 MINS**

6 tbsp olive oil, plus extra for greasing

juice of 1 lemon

4 tbsp finely chopped flat-leaf parsley

½–1 tsp chilli powder or ½–1 tsp Tabasco

4 swordfish steaks, about 225g (8oz) each, deboned, skinned and cut into 2.5cm (1in) cubes

2 orange, yellow or red peppers, cored, deseeded and cut into 2.5cm (1in) pieces

For the green salsa:

1 bunch rocket or parsley, finely chopped

2 garlic cloves, crushed, or 1 tsp garlic puree

8 tbsp olive oil

4 tbsp balsamic vinegar

salt and pepper

1 With a fork, whisk together the olive oil, lemon juice, parsley and chilli powder or Tabasco in a large non-metallic bowl. Add the swordfish pieces and gently cover with the marinade. Cover and marinate for 20 minutes in a chilled cool box.

2 Meanwhile, make the green salsa by whisking together the chopped rocket or parsley leaves, garlic, olive oil, and vinegar and season with salt and pepper. Set aside.

3 Grease 8 metal skewers and thread the fish and peppers onto the skewers. Place in a grilling cage if you have one and grill over a barbecue of campfire for 5–8 minutes, or until the fish is cooked through and begins to flake. Serve with the green salsa.

Mediterranean-style grilled prawns

This recipe can be made with frozen or fresh tiger prawns. If using frozen, allow another 3–4 minutes cooking time

SERVES 4
TIME TO COOK **8 MINS**

2 tbsps olive oil

juice of 2 lemons (and a little of the rind from one half if possible)

2 garlic cloves crushed, or ½ tsp garlic paste

6 sprigs of thyme, or small bunch of parsley, basil or oregano, chopped

drop of Tabasco

salt and pepper

24 large pacific or tiger prawns with shells on (frozen are fine)

1 Mix the olive oil, lemon juice, lemon rind and garlic together in a bowl large enough to hold the prawns. Add the chopped herbs, Tabasco, salt and pepper and combine.

2 Now add the prawns and coat them in the olive oil. Leave to stand for 5 minutes.

3 Thread the prawns onto oiled metal skewers and place in the grilling cage. Hold one side over the campfire flame until they turn pink (about 3–5 minutes). Keep them above the flames so that they do not burn.

4 Turn the cage over and grill the other side for another 3 minutes or so until the prawn shells are pink all the way round.

Honey mustard barbecued chicken

If you haven't time to marinade the chicken, just glaze it

SERVES **4**
TIME TO COOK **30 MINS**

8 chicken drumsticks or thighs

120ml (4fl oz) tomato ketchup

2 tbsp olive oil

120ml (4fl oz) orange juice

60ml (2fl oz) balsamic vinegar

1 tsp dried oregano

¼ tsp freshly ground black pepper

1 garlic clove, crushed

For the glaze:
2 tbsp clear honey

2 tbsp wholegrain mustard

zest of 1 lemon

1 Make 2 or 3 cuts into each chicken portion and place in a large bowl. Make the marinade by mixing the tomato ketchup, olive oil, orange juice, vinegar, oregano, pepper, and garlic in a bowl. Coat the chicken evenly and leave to marinate for 20 minutes in a chilled cool box.

2 Remove the chicken from the marinade. Barbecue or grill over the campfire for 15 minutes, turning once.

5 Combine the honey, mustard, and lemon zest to make a glaze, and brush it onto the chicken.

6 Cook for a further 10–15 minutes, turning frequently, or until cooked through. To test, pierce with a knife – the juices should run clear and the meat should no longer be pink.

The barbecue coals or fire embers should have turned white before you begin cooking

Lamb brochettes

Cook these lamb skewers quickly to keep the meat pink and tender

SERVES **4**
TIME TO COOK **8 MINS**

2 tbsp ground coriander

4 garlic cloves, crushed, or
1 tsp garlic puree

7 tbsp olive oil

2 tsp clear honey

1 tsp grated lemon zest

salt and pepper

1kg (2¼lb) lamb, cut
into chunks

For the vinaigrette:
2 tbsp red wine vinegar

6 tbsp chopped coriander
leaves

5 ripe tomatoes, chopped

1 Put the ground coriander in a bowl and stir in half the garlic, add 3 tablespoons of the olive oil, half the honey, the lemon zest, and pepper to taste. Coat the lamb with the rub, and marinate in a bowl for 20 minutes in a a chilled coolbox.

2 To make the vinaigrette, use a fork to whisk the remaining oil, vinegar, and fresh coriander in a bowl, stir in the tomatoes, and set aside.

3 Remove the meat from the marinade and thread onto oiled metal skewers, season with salt, place in the grilling cage, and grill over the campfire or barbecue for 8 minutes, or until evenly browned. Serve with the tomato vinaigrette.

Deli steak sandwich

This sandwich can be made simply with steak and salad, or given added depth with cheeses, horseradish, and dill pickles

SERVES **4**

TIME TO COOK **4 MINS**

4 crusty white rolls or small baguettes, split in half

4 rump steaks or sirloin steaks,140g (5oz) each

2 tbsp oil

salt and pepper

2 tsp creamed horseradish (optional)

115g (4oz) cream cheese (optional)

115g (4oz) blue cheese, such as Stilton or Roquefort, crumbled (optional)

4 lettuce leaves

2 tomatoes, sliced

1 tbsp mustard

1 onion, thinly sliced into rings

8 dill pickle slices (optional)

1 Lay the cut sides of the bread on the pan and lightly toast them in batches on a heated ridged cast-iron grill pan or in the grilling cage. Remove the bread from the pan and set aside.

2 Brush the steaks with oil, season to taste with salt and pepper, and cook for 3–4 minutes on each side in the grill pan or grilling cage.

3 Meanwhile, mix together the creamed horseradish, cream cheese, and blue cheese. Spread the mixture on to the toasted sides of the bread, then lay the lettuce leaves and tomato slices on the bottom halves.

4 When the steaks are cooked, divide them between the bread rolls, add a little mustard to each, and pile onion rings and pickle slices on top. Replace the lids and serve.

Skewered beef with lime, ginger, and honey

Skewered meats are perfect for the barbecue or campfire

SERVES **4**

TIME TO COOK **20 MINS**

5cm (2in) fresh root ginger, peeled and grated

juice of 1 lime

1 tbsp light soy sauce

1 tbsp honey

1 tbsp olive oil

3 spring onions, roughly chopped

500g (1lb 2oz) beef fillet or sirloin,cut into 2.5cm (1in) cubes

16 cherry tomatoes

salt and pepper

1 Place the ginger, lime juice, soy sauce, honey, olive oil, and spring onions in a bowl. Add the beef pieces, and coat in the marinade, then leave to marinate for 20 minutes in a well chilled cool box.

2 Thread the meat onto the oiled metal skewers, putting 2 cherry tomatoes on each skewer. Place the skewers in a grilling cage (if you have one) and quickly grill over a barbecue or the campfire.

3 Cook the beef skewers for 2–4 minutes on each side, or until well-coloured but still pink inside.

Cubed lamb steaks work just as well if beef is unavailable

Make at home

If you are travelling to your destination by car, consider making a stew, casserole, or hearty soup at home before you go camping, so at least the first campsite meal is "ready-made". Then all you have to do when you get there is reheat it.

Remember to keep food properly chilled in a cool box during transportation. And if you freeze it before your journey, the dish must be thoroughly defrosted before it is reheated. When reheating, bring the dish to the boil and simmer for at least 10 minutes before serving.

Sweet treats such as apple muffins, flapjacks, and banana bread are ideal for making in advance, and taking along with you for picnics or simple puddings in the evening.

Hearty bean soup

Pasta, beans, and vegetables make this soup a satisfying meal

SERVES **4**
TIME TO COOK **40 MINS**
REHEAT TIME **8 MINS**

2 tbsp olive oil

2 celery sticks, finely chopped

2 carrots, finely chopped

1 onion, finely chopped

400g (14oz) can of white cannellini beans, drained

400g (14oz) can chopped tomatoes

750ml (1¼ pints) chicken or vegetable stock

salt and pepper

60g (2oz) small short-cut pasta

4 tbsp flat-leaf parsley, chopped

40g (1½oz) Parmesan cheese, finely grated

1 Heat the oil in a large pan over a medium heat. Add the celery, carrots, and onion and fry, stirring occasionally, for 5 minutes, or until tender. Stir in the drained beans, the tomatoes with their juice, the stock, and season to taste with salt and pepper. Bring to the boil, stirring, then cover and leave to simmer for 20 minutes.

2 Add the pasta and simmer for a further 10–12 minutes, or until cooked but still tender to the bite.

3 To reheat at the campsite, bring to the boil and then simmer for 5 minutes. Stir in the parsley and half the Parmesan, then adjust the seasoning. Serve hot, sprinkled with the remaining Parmesan.

Navarin of lamb

A complete one-pot meal, this can be chilled or frozen and reheated

SERVES **4**
TIME TO COOK **1HR 15 MINS**
REHEAT TIME **18 MINS**

15g (½oz) butter

1 tbsp olive oil

900g (2lb) middle neck of lamb, cut into pieces

2 small onions, quartered

1 tbsp plain flour

400ml (14fl oz) lamb stock or beef stock

2 tbsp tomato purée

1 bouquet garni

salt and pepper

300g (10oz) small new potatoes

300g (10oz) small whole carrots

300g (10oz) baby turnips

175g (6oz) French beans

1 Melt the butter with the oil in a large flameproof casserole, add the lamb, and fry until brown on all sides. Add the onions and fry gently for 5 minutes, stirring frequently.

2 Sprinkle the flour over the meat and stir well for 2 minutes, or until the pieces are evenly coated. Stir in the stock, add the tomato purée and bouquet garni, and season with salt and pepper. Bring to the boil, then cover and simmer for 45 minutes.

3 Add the potatoes, carrots, and turnips. Cover and cook for a further 15 minutes.

4 To reheat at the campsite, bring to the boil, then stir in the beans, cover, and simmer for a further 10–15 minutes, or until all the vegetables are tender. Serve with chunks of French bread to soak up the juices.

Hungarian goulash

Serve this rich, warming stew with any dried pasta

SERVES **4**
TIME TO COOK **2HRS**
REHEAT TIME **20 MINS**

4 tbsp oil

900g (2lb) braising steak, cut into 2.5cm (1in) cubes

2 large onions, thinly sliced

2 garlic cloves, crushed

2 red peppers, deseeded and chopped

1 tbsp paprika, plus extra to garnish

400g (14oz) can chopped tomatoes

2 tbsp tomato purée

1 tbsp plain flour

300ml (10fl oz) beef stock

1 tsp chopped, fresh thyme

salt and pepper

150ml (5fl oz) soured cream

1 Preheat the oven to 160°C (325°F/Gas 3).

2 Heat half the oil in a large frying pan and brown the meat in batches, transferring to a large casserole as each batch finish browning.

3 Add the remaining oil to the pan, lower the heat, and fry the onions, garlic, and peppers until soft. Stir in the paprika and cook for 1 minute, then add the tomatoes and purée. Mix the flour with a little stock until smooth, then pour it into the pan with the rest of the stock. Bring to the boil, stirring often. Add the thyme, season, then pour the sauce into the casserole.

4 Cover tightly and place in the oven for 2 hours or until the beef is tender.

5 To reheat at the campsite, simmer gently for 20 minutes. Top each serving of goulash with a couple of spoonfuls of soured cream and a sprinkle of paprika.

Banana bread

This moist cake keeps for up to a week in an airtight container

SERVES **4**
TIME TO COOK **1HR**
15 MINS

250g (9oz) self-raising flour

½ tsp baking powder

85g (3oz) butter, plus extra for greasing

150g (5½oz) light muscovado sugar

3 ripe bananas

100ml (3½fl oz) plain yogurt

2 eggs

85g (3oz) walnuts, chopped (optional)

1 Preheat the oven to 180°C (350°F/ Gas 4). Sift the flour and baking powder together into a mixing bowl and rub in the butter until the mixture resembles fine breadcrumbs. Stir in the sugar.

2 Mash the bananas with a fork, then add to the flour with the yogurt, eggs, and walnuts (if using). Beat with a wooden spoon until well combined. Spoon into a greased, lined loaf tin, level the top, and make a slight dip in the centre.

3 Bake for 1–1¼ hours, or until a skewer inserted into the centre comes out clean. Leave to cool in the tin for 5 minutes, then turn out on to a wire rack to cool completely.

Apple muffins

A home-baked treat for breakfast

MAKES **12**
TIME TO COOK **25 MINS**

1 green apple, peeled and chopped

2 tsp lemon juice

115g (4oz) light demerara sugar, plus extra for sprinkling

200g (7oz) plain flour

85g (3oz) wholemeal flour

4 tsp baking powder

1 tbsp ground mixed spice

½ tsp salt

60g (2oz) pecan nuts, chopped (optional)

250ml (8fl oz) milk

4 tbsp sunflower oil

1 egg, beaten

1 Preheat the oven to 200°C (400°F/ Gas 6). Line a 12-hole American-style muffin tin with paper cases and set aside. Put the apple in a bowl, add the lemon juice, and toss. Add 4 tbsp of the sugar and set aside for 5 minutes.

2 Meanwhile, sift the plain and wholemeal flours, baking powder, mixed spice, and salt into a large bowl, tipping in any bran left in the sieve. Stir in the remaining sugar and pecans (if using) then make a well in the centre of the dry ingredients.

3 Beat together the milk, oil, and egg, then add the apple. Tip the wet ingredients into the centre of the dry ingredients and mix together lightly to make a lumpy batter.

4 Spoon the mixture into the paper cases, filling each case three-quarters full. Bake the muffins for 20–25 minutes, or until the tops are peaked and brown. Cool and sprinkle with extra sugar. Keep in an airtight box.

Flapjacks

These are simple to make with just a few storecupboard ingredients

MAKES **16-20**

TIME TO COOK **40 MINS**

225g (8oz) butter, plus extra for greasing

225g (8oz) light soft brown sugar

2 tbsp golden syrup

350g (12oz) rolled oats

1 Preheat the oven to 150°C (300°F/ Gas 2). Lightly grease a square cake tin.

2 Put the butter, sugar, and syrup in a large saucepan and heat over a medium-low heat until the butter has melted. Remove the pan from the heat and stir in the oats.

3 Transfer the mixture to the prepared tin and press down firmly. Bake for 40 minutes, or until evenly golden and just beginning to brown at the edges

4 Leave to cool for 10 minutes, then cut into 16 squares, or 20 rectangles. Leave in the tin until completely cooled. Store in an airtight container.

Epilogue: Striking camp

The success of your next camping trip rests with how you finish the last one. As tempting as it is to throw everything together and forget about it, sorting gear out, checking it for wear and tear, cleaning things, and storing them properly will save you time in the future. Begin by taking down your tent. Ideally, it will be dry, but if not, don't worry, you'll need to air it when you get home anyway.

1 A firmly seated tent peg can be awkward to get out of the ground, especially if it's been there for some time. Use another peg to hook under the stuck one.

2 While you're taking out the pegs, don't forget to slacken the buckles on any tapes you've tightened to improve the pitching of the tent. This will make it much easier to put up next time.

Fold the guy ropes up neatly so that they won't get tangled while the tent is stored. You'll then be able to undo them easily next time you go camping.

3

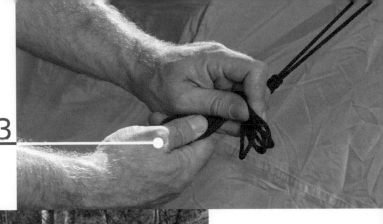

4 Don't be tempted to pull the tent poles out of their sleeves. You'll only separate the pole segments, which will make the job harder. Push them through instead.

You don't have to be obsessive about folding your tent, because it's a good idea to air it when you get home to drive out any moisture that may remain. If your tent is folded up so that it fits in the bag, it's good enough.

5

Useful resources

UK and Ireland

Alan Rogers Booking for European campsites.
www.alanrogers.com

Blacks Stores in major UK cities.
www.blacks.co.uk

Camping and Caravanning Club Over 4000 campsites in the UK and abroad. Advice and monthly magazine.
www.campingandcaravanningclub.co.uk

Camping International Tent specialist in South East England and online.
www.camping-intl.com

Camping magazine Practical information and equipment reviews.
www.outandaboutlive.co.uk

Canoe Camping Club Organization that combines the pleasures of canoeing with camping.
www.canoecampingclub.co.uk

Cotswold Outdoor See right.

Council for National Parks Organisation campaigning for the protection of the UK national park system www.cnp.org.uk

Go Camping UK Holidays in pre-pitched tents.
www.gocampinguk.co.uk

Go Outdoor Ireland Camping kit and other outdoor gear. Ships worldwide.
www.gooutdoorireland.com

Go Outdoors Retail branches throughout England and online shop.
www.gooutdoors.co.uk

Lancashire Sports Repairs Alterations and repairs for outdoor equipment.
www.lsr.gb.com

LPM Bohemia Makers and sellers of luxury yurts. www.lpmbohemia.com

Mountain Bothies Association Manages and maintains the mostly Scottish network of bothies, free shelters in Britain's wildest areas.
www.mountainbothies.org.uk

Outdoorgear UK Large choice of tents, sleeping gear, packs and accessories.
www.outdoorgear.co.uk

Ramblers' Association Campaigns for the rights of walkers in the UK.
www.ramblers.org.uk

Scottish Camping Scottish campsites.
www.scottishcamping.com

Scottish Mountain Gear Repairs and manufactures fabric-based outdoor equipment, including tents.
www.scottishmountaingear.com

Snow+Rock Climbing and skiing specialists with camping department.
www.snowandrock.com

TGO magazine Advice for walkers.
www.tgomagazine.co.uk

Tiso Scottish outdoor specialists with both high street and online outlets.
www.tiso.com

Tent 2 Hire Tent rental company supplying the whole UK.
www.tent2hire.co.uk

Trek Hire UK Based in Surrey, this company rents expedition clothing and equipment.
www.trek-hire.co.uk

Trellyn Woodland Campsite For serious glampers. www.trellyn.co.uk

www.ukcampsite.co.uk Guide to campsites in the UK.

UK National Parks Practical advice on camping in the UK
www.nationalparks.gov.uk

Wild Camping Advice
www.mountaineering-scotland.org.

WildDay.com Cooking equip. tents and accessories for UK and Ireland.
www.wildday.co.uk

YHA/Camping Barns
www.yha.org.uk

Australia and New Zealand

Activate Outdoors Sydney-based store with a comprehensive online range.
www.activateoutdoors.com.au

Green Coast Shop based in Auckland.
www.greencoast.co.nz

Kathmandu Shops in New Zealand, Australia and the UK, plus online store.
www.kathmandu.co.nz

Paddy Pallin Stores all over Australia, and a wide online range.
www.paddypallin.com.au

Outdoors.com.au Tents, backpacks and equipment online and from the Melbourne store.
www.outdoors.com.au

Oztrail Tents online from the manufacturer or stockists.
www.oztrail.com.au

NZ Campsite Camping gear for hire, including cooking equipment.
www.nzcampsite.co.nz

Snowgum Online store and branches in Australia and New Zealand.
www.snowgum.com.au

Summit Gear Shop online with the outdoor equipment manufacturers or visit the NSW stores.
www.summitgear.com.au

USA

US National Parks Information for campsites in US national parks.
www.nps.gov

Sierra Club Matching outdoor instruction and advice, with razor sharp environmental campaigning.
www.sierraclub.org

Backpacker magazine Useful source of information and advice on camping.
www.backpacker.com

Camping.com An online magazine and resource. www.camping.com

Family Camping Gear
A practical site packed with information for families going camping for the first time.
www.familycampinggear.com

Cotswold Outdoor

Cotswold Outdoor stock one of the most comprehensive ranges of outdoor clothing and equipment in the UK. Everything from tents and cooking gear to gadgets and accessories. A highly successful specialist retailer, Cotswold Outdoor have over 30 stores distributed throughout the UK. Their award-winning website runs an efficient online order service that allows you to shop by brand or department. They deliver to destinations worldwide, including North America, Europe and Australasia.

www.cotswoldoutdoor.com
Tel: 0870 442 7755

Index

Acknowledgments

Ed and Kate Douglas wish to thank Editor Claire Tennant-Scull, Designer Will Hicks and Dawn Henderson and Mary-Clare Jerram at Dorling Kindersley for making this book such a pleasure to write. We'd also like to thank our children Rosa and Joe for humouring us on so many camping trips over the years, and making us look again at the way the world is.

Sue Hughes wishes to thank fellow camp cook Angie McKenna for her enthusiasm and contributions.

Dorling Kindersley wish to thank Caroline Fanshawe and Sue Hughes for suggesting the idea for this book; Tarik Mirza and Matt Farrar from Cotswold Outdoor for being so helpful throughout the project; John from LPM Bohemia – The Tent Co Ltd for kindly giving us a photograph; Debajyoti Datta for the illustrations; Nicky Collings for Art Direction; Simon Murrell for Design; Annie Nicholls for Food Styling; Hilary Bird for the Index.

Picture credits The publisher would like to thank the following for their kind permission to reproduce their photographs:
(Key: a-above; b-below/bottom; c-centre; l-left; r-right; t-top) Page: 2 Axiom Photographic Agency:
Ian Cumming. 4–5 Getty Images: Michael DeYoung. 6 Photolibrary: Ken Gillham (br). 8–9 Corbis: Solus-Veer. 14 Getty Images: Peter Hannert. 22 Robert Harding Picture Library: Walter Rawlings. 24 Getty Images: Jim Dyson. 26 Getty Images: Dennis Drenner. 28 Getty Images: Lars Schneider. 33 iStockphoto.com: Jill Lang. 48 Courtesy Coleman / Campingaz: (bl). 48–49 Courtesy Coleman / Campingaz: (c). 56 Photolibrary: Fancy (br); FoodCollection (tl); Michael J. Hippie (bl); IPS Photo Index (tr). 62 DK Images: Julian Baker. 84 Alamy Images: Bon Appetit. 90–91 Photolibrary: Ken Gillham. 92 Photolibrary: Per Klaesson. 96 Photolibrary: Monkey Business Images Ltd. 113 Getty Images: Justin Bailie. 114 Alamy Images: Eddie Gerald (r); imagebroker (l); A. T. Willett (c). 115 Alamy Images: Phil Degginger (tl); Jim Henderson (tr) (br); Steve Shuey (bl). 116 Till Credner , Allthesky.com. 119 Till Credner , Allthesky.com. 122 Photolibrary: Hans-Peter Merten / Mauritius. 124 Photolibrary: Banana Stock. 136 Getty Images: Michael Jungblut All other images © Dorling Kindersley For further information see: www.dkimages.com